BRIGH

CW01510540

GERMINAL
BY
ÉMILE ZOLA

Intelligent Education

INFLUENCE PUBLISHERS

Nashville, Tennessee

BRIGHT NOTES: Germinal
www.BrightNotes.com

ISBN: 978-1-645421-06-1 (Paperback)
ISBN: 978-1-645421-07-8 (eBook)

Published in accordance with the U.S. Copyright Office Orphan Works and Mass Digitization report of the register of copyrights, June 2015.

Originally published by Monarch Press.
Carolyn Roberts Welch, 1974
2019 Edition published by Influence Publishers.

Interior design by Lapiz Digital Services. Cover Design by Thinkpen Designs.

Printed in the United States of America.

Library of Congress Cataloging-in-Publication Data forthcoming.
Names: Intelligent Education
Title: BRIGHT NOTES: Germinal
Subject: STU004000 STUDY AIDS / Book Notes

CONTENTS

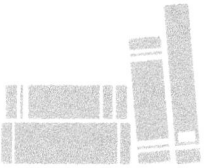

INTRODUCTION TO EMILE ZOLA

One might judiciously begin a compendium on Emile Zola's *Germinal* with a discretionary note concerning what some might consider to be sinister elements of Socialist or Communist sympathy in Zola's work, plus a discretionary remark relating to certain elements of plot material and description which people of extremely mild sensibilities might consider to be obscene. *Germinal* is based almost entirely on coal mine actualities, and as college-level material, it seems inconceivable that alleged obscenity could be actually considered as an operable issue in its study, particularly in this permissive era in which books which actually are of questionable merit are permeating the academic climate. Due to the weight of its content, however, *Germinal* would not be recommended by this commentator for secondary school students, with the possible exception of advanced groups.

Despite any reservations rooted in the sensibilities which one might have concerning *Germinal* or the Rougon-Macquart, one would have to concede that Zola's thirteenth novel of the cycle is a masterpiece of rage and is perhaps one of the angriest books ever written. A literary blast-furnace of smoldering fury, *Germinal* forms a nearly perfect blend of Zola's scientific view of history, his documented actualities from his celebrated preliminary sketches or "ebauches," his mastery of myth and symbol, and his perception of apocalypse. This volume will concern itself with these elements as well as with certain social, political, and economic forces which were at work in France during the Second Empire (1852–1870) from the "coup d'etat" to the Sedan disaster.

It is basically this epoch and its effects that form the chronological superstructure and inner plot material for the twenty-novel Rougon-Macquart cycle. Among the economic forces that were at work in France during the Second Empire, particular note should be taken of the rise of the merciless industrial bourgeoisie, the rise of labor exploitation, and the solidification of these groups into eventual power blocks: the "laissez-faire" capitalistic monopolies versus the rising discontented proletariat **foreshadowing** organized labor. This study of *Germinal* includes detailed analysis of such foreign influences as Germany's Karl Marx, London's International Workingmen's Association, and Russia's pre-Bolshevik anarchists. All of these elements play important roles in the genesis, gestation, and resolution of the *Germinal* plot and background, and the mastery of Emile Zola lies in his ability to treat all of this material with a high degree of political impartiality and yet with unsurpassed literary insight and artistry.

It is ironic that many of the horrors manifest in Emile Zola's *Germinal*, such as cave-in potential and firedamp menace, are still prevalent today in coal mines in what would otherwise seem to be a highly enlightened and socially conscious United States. With the exception of Upton Sinclair's *King Coal*, there has been a conspicuous absence of American novels dealing with coal mining. Interestingly, there has been no masterpiece from our country on this subject even approaching the stature of *Germinal*, thus giving Zola's novel high priority in relevance.

INTRODUCTION TO THE AUTHOR

One may derive an accurate picture of Emile Edouard Charles Antoine Zola's life and times (April 2, 1840-September 29, 1902) by examining the detailed chronology which follows, but there are various other equally important biographical factors which defy the delineations of a timetable. Much has been written on Emile Zola's life, much of it being oversentimentalized with frequently an overemphasis of the Dreyfus Affair. There was even a motion picture released in 1937, starring Paul Muni, dealing with the life of the author, not an inferior picture but bearing conspicuous elements of pro-Dreyfus hero-worship. A certain element of this hero-worship factor may also be found in the otherwise excellent and authoritative biography of Zola by Ernest Vizetelly, the son of Henry Vizetelly, Zola's closest English friend who put his well-established printing career at stake in his inhospitably received English translations of the Rougon-Macquart working-class novels, especially *La Terre* (The Earth).

So far as academic objectivity is concerned, the most authoritative English language biographies of Emile Zola in existence today are those by F. W. J. Hemmings, Elliott M. Grant, and Angus Wilson. The biography by Hemmings includes thorough perspectives of the Rougon-Macquart novels in terms of influences, artistic conception, and literary criticism. That by Grant, Professor of French, Emeritus, from Williams College, includes the details of actual events and social documents recorded in Zola's journals, which formed the rough preliminary sketches or "ebauches" of the novels, as well as compressed, concise biography. Wilson's biography is more psychologically oriented than the aforementioned works and includes references to such intimate biographical details as Zola's relationship with his mother. So far as English language biography is concerned, one other source-work worthy of examination is the highly detailed and interestingly written biography by the nineteenth-century historical specialist Matthew Josephson.

ZOLA'S EXPERIENCE WITH ECONOMIC DISTRESS

Basically, a brief approach to Emile Zola's life would include mention of six preeminent turning points, focusing on the following course-altering events. The first would be the death of Zola's father when the boy was only six years old, with the subsequent inevitable reduction of his mother's financial circumstances. This event had the effect of breaking the author's idyllic childhood at the sunny and poetically inspiring Aix-en-Provence and taking him to Paris with his mother and grandmother where he had eventually to see family furniture carried out of the house due to financial need. Emile's mother had come of proud northern French peasant stock from Dourdan, and one of her most obsessive dreads was that of ever becoming part of the poverty-stricken economic lower class for which she had so much ingrained contempt. It was in his early exposure to certain attitudes toward the poor, as well as his direct experience of dire poverty itself in his early manhood, that Zola became the literary master of the miseries of the working class. Not only did Zola develop interesting attitudes toward the poor, but he came also to develop equally interesting and all-consuming attitudes toward the bourgeoisie. The author himself came to lack any personal sense of class identity: he had bourgeois roots but had become poor, not being able to identify himself with either class. He had been brought up by his mother to have contempt for the unrefined masses and at the same time gained a well-founded contempt for the devious bourgeois lawyers and business associates of his deceased father who literally cheated his mother out of money from the Aix canal project to which she was rightfully entitled. In addition to these specific biographical facts, there was likewise a feeling of proletarian revolution in the air during Zola's lifetime, particularly the early part which brought the Revolution in France of 1848, and the immediate and rapid succession of Marxist meetings and documents which were to permeate Paris.

ZOLA'S ACADEMIC FAILURES

As well as experiencing the shock and responsibility incurred by his father's sudden death in 1847, a second turning point manifested itself in the years 1859 and 1860 in his twice failing his baccalaureate examinations, eliminating him from major professional considerations and giving him an enormous sense of failure, particularly to his mother who had had educational aspirations for her son. Facing the most squalid destitution of his life, Zola took a menial job on the Paris docks. His mother received support from his grandmother (her mother) until she died, but another, more favorable turning point presented itself to the young man at this time. In 1862, Emile Zola was given a job as a sales clerk with the Hachette publishing house of Paris, and then eventually gained a position as a publicity chief. Zola still lived in poverty during this time, but his imminent success as a commercial writer was becoming evident.

FRANCE'S FIRST BEST-SELLING AUTHOR

As he began to write on increasingly controversial subjects in his stories for *Hachette,* he approached his third major crossroads in 1866. It was an ultimatum by the manager concerning police inquiries about *La Confession de Claude* (The Confession of Claude): either to stop writing so sensationally or to sever connections with *Hachette*. The young author decided to leave the strictures of *Hachette's* company and to devote his life to writing, about which he had learned so much through direct contact with the behind-the-scenes intrigues of the publishing world's back rooms. Zola learned of what stuff commercial success was made and literally turned himself into a businesslike writing-machine, not letting a single day pass without turning out some measure of prose. While affluent writers like Marcel Proust wrote for the exclusive salons and could afford to have early books published at their own expense, Emile Zola became the novelist of the public press, gathering actualities for his plots by mingling with the incredibly poor, and being the first French author to sell his books in the hundreds of thousands. He wrote about virtually every sector of business enterprise in his Rougon-Macquart novels, and it never ceases to arouse this commentator's curiosity as to why Zola did not write a novel set in a publishing milieu.

ZOLA AS FATHER

The fourth major turning point of Zola's life occurred in 1880 after his marriage, which was childless. This particular event was a trauma and was to haunt Zola for the larger part of his subsequent life. The author, his mother, and his wife lived together, and after a series of domestic difficulties, his mother died. The author experienced psychic breakdown after this event, and for a long time he produced morbidly depressing stories like *La Joie de Vivre* (The Joy of Living).

Zola was ambitious, his mother proud and humiliated, and his wife gentle and long suffering. Sadly, Zola was to turn away from the morbid atmosphere of the home that he had associated with his wife and was to have two children, a son and a daughter, by a younger mistress. His wife was initially furious but took the responsibility of adopting the children herself and took care of them after Zola's death.

The fifth turning point of Emile Zola's life virtually sounded the death knell for Zola as a literary master. With his new female acquaintance and the refreshment and delight of children, the author's once tremendous literary power disintegrated and atrophied. Adversity had brought fruit to Zola's genius, giving to his work that enormous sense of scale and extraordinary virtuosity that often only misery and grief can bring to a writer. After the completion of the Rougon-Macquart cycle, Emile Zola would have probably receded into complete obscurity had not political events in France taken the course they did at the end of the nineteenth century.

ZOLA'S "J'ACCUSE"

The Dreyfus Affair brought as much if not more posthumous fame to Emile Zola as the entirety of the Rougon-Macquart cycle. Had it not been for the author's inordinate courage in his published open letter to the sixth President of the French Third Republic, Francois Felix Faure, the Alsaceborn Jew, Alfred Dreyfus, would probably never have been cleared of the treason charges leveled against him by the government. Dreyfus was an army officer convicted of selling French classified military data to Germany, under what has been considered by many as circumstantial evidence, and sentenced to the French penal colony on Devil's Island. Zola's celebrated letter of January 13, 1898 became known as "J'Accuse" because of the frequent repetition of the phrase throughout it. Its content denounced the conviction of Alfred Dreyfus and called for immediate rectification of what the writer considered to be a miscarriage of justice. At the same time, Zola dared the French government to prosecute him for his public charges. Prosecution was, in fact, begun against Zola, and on February 23, 1898, Zola was convicted of libeling the military authorities and was sentenced to pay a 5,000-franc fine and to serve a six-month prison sentence. Zola appealed the verdict and obtained a retrial, but was again condemned.

ZOLA A NATIONAL HERO

In the meantime, through the help of his friends, Zola managed to defect to England where he received help from his friend, Henry Vizetelly, and remained in hiding. Zola returned to France a short time later by a petition set forth by Marcel Proust and Anatole France, and was eventually celebrated as a national hero championing human rights. It was primarily through the risky efforts of Emile Zola that it was eventually demonstrated that the documents on which the conviction of Dreyfus had been obtained had been forged. In 1900, a new French ministry sponsored a bill granting amnesty to all parties unjustly accused in the Dreyfus case.

The publicity drawn by the Dreyfus controversy had ugly overtones of anti-Semitism and polarized France into two ardently hateful camps, the liberal pro-Dreyfusards and the conservative anti-Dreyfusards. Likewise, Emile Zola died under what many have considered to be suspicious circumstances: he died from asphyxiation resulting from a clogged fireplace flue soon after his firm stand on unpopular aspects of the Dreyfus issue. No one knows for certain as to whether or not homicidal intent was involved in the chimney clogging, but the author was hailed a national hero at his funeral. The cry "Germinal!" which repeatedly rose into the air on that occasion has augmented the reputation of the thirteenth Rougon-Macquart novel, Emile Zola's most celebrated novel.

INTRODUCTION TO EMILE ZOLA

PHILOSOPHICAL INFLUENCES ON ZOLA

. . . .

Among the extra-literary luminaries from the world of philosophy and criticism to be of monumental influence upon Emile Zola were such men, among others, as Hippolyte Taine, Auguste Comte, Charles Darwin, and Karl Marx.

TAINE'S INFLUENCE

Taine systematized and developed various earlier theories of heredity and environment and hoped to make literary criticism a science. As all integral parts of a scientific organism were to maintain certain necessary connections, so too all the parts of a work, a man, or a period were to form one scientific system, every system having its own dominant characteristics. Taine had proposed to examine all the variations of given literary data as influenced by what he called "race" ("heredity"), "milieu" ("environment"), and "moment" ("period"): literature was to be the document of a particular society in a certain age. Methodologically, Taine applied the laws of natural science to human science. It was in this spirit that Emile Zola pursued his own Naturalistic method in his Rougon-Macquart novels, his scientifically oriented history of a family under the Second Empire. Among Hippolyte Taine's finest critical works are the *Essais de Critique et d'Histoire* (Essays of Criticism and of History) of 1857, the *Nouveaux Essais* (New Essays) of 1865, the polemic in *Les Philosophies Francais du XIX Siecle* (French Philosophies of the 19th Century), and the causal study *Les Origines de la France Contemporaine* (Origins of Contemporary France), published in separate parts between 1875 and 1890.

COMTE'S INFLUENCE

It was Auguste Comte whose *Cours de Philosophie Positive* (Course of Positivist Philosophy) of 1830, and whose *Systeme de Philosophie Positive* (System of Positivist Philosophy) of 1857, gave special importance to a new spirit in literature-that of the inductive or investigative process as a literary aesthetic, this spirit of hypothesis yielding scores of novels utilizing demonstrative evidence as the basis of their plot lines. As well as influencing Emile Zola's novels, the Comte consciousness spread into a large body of non-French writings through the influence of John Stuart Mill and Herbert Spencer, two English philosophers heavily indebted to Auguste Comte. Among non-French novelists influenced by Comte were those whose numerous works of fiction bore the evidence-oriented overtones of "scientisme" in their early science fiction and detective investigation novels, such as those by H. G. Wells, Edgar Allan Poe, and Sir Arthur Conan Doyle.

Fiction was being regarded as a social science in itself, with whole strata of society being examined in the spirit of Comte's Positivism. This close microscopic scrutiny, however, inevitably led to a highly graphic realization of the disparity between the real and the ideal in society. Ultimately, as in Emile Zola's Rougon-Macquart novels, society was to be presented as some malevolent mechanism, a mechanical monster growing out of the Industrial Revolution and its diversified conglomerate of mass culture. The relentless momentum of this runaway mechanization and progress obsession was to have a profound effect on man's sense of dignity, his hopes, and his sense of group "consciousness."

Basically Auguste Comte's Positivism involved the following: he believed that religion and metaphysics were obsolete, and that philosophy had passed through two full stages, the theological ("l'etat theologique"), and the **metaphysical** ("l'etat metaphysique") into a third current stage imbued with science, the positivistic stage ("l'etat positif"). From this scientific stage onward, man's thinking would be based on the positivistic study of facts and will lead him to discover the natural laws of phenomena. Auguste Comte's influence was to first spread to such scientists as Louis Pasteur and Claude Bernard, then to novelists such as Emile Zola. It is Comte who is credited with making Sociology a science ("la sociologique"), and like certain more radical political scientists, Comte denied religion, venerated the 1789 French Revolution, and looked for a new political order.

DARWIN'S INFLUENCE

In the genesis and evolution of **Realism** and Naturalism, Charles Darwin's *The Origin of Species* was significant due to its placing of man on the conveyor belt of scientifically conceived machine-like articles. Its primary significance to literature lay in its placing of heredity and environment as controlling factors in the determination of human character and conduct. Darwin's influence was felt in virtually all the disciplines, ranging from the philosophical spirit of *Also Sprach Zarathustra* (Thus Spoke Zarathustra) of 1883, and *Jenseits von Gut und Bose* (Between Good and Evil) of 1886, by Friedrich Nietzsche, to the plays of Henrik Ibsen and the novels of Emile Zola, in which representation of heredity and environment are principal concerns in the evolution of modern life and thought.

MARX'S INFLUENCE

It was in conjunction with the influence of Charles Darwin that Karl Marx's thought also gave impetus to scientific applications of socialism in Naturalistic literature. *The Communist Manifesto* of 1847 was compounded with Das Kapital of 1867–1894 as influential economic theory, through the application of Darwin's concept of the survival of the fittest, of natural selection, in an economic context. In the inevitable rise of Socialism, Marx theorized that the capitalistic system would ultimately wane away and destroy itself; it would fall to the wayside and not survive. Emile Zola's *Germinal* touches upon this idea by placing his gruesome story of a mine strike during an economic recession. The new Marxist literature was, in the spirit of "scientisme," to become an objectified and scientific instrument of social criticism and reform. With the spread of deterministic Marxist economic ideology, especially in France which seemed to be its seeding ground, the Naturalistic writers absorbed nascent Marxism with the idea that human misery came not of a Classical tragic flaw in an autonomous tragic hero, but of socio-economic forces that reduce human beings to victims. Unfortunately, many of the later Marxist writers became propagandists advocating some kind of control over these determined forces, often sapping the Marxist school of its original creative energy.

Perhaps the most conspicuous element of Marxist influence in Emile Zola's Rougon-Macquart novels is his collective group consciousness. His scientific forces of heredity, environment, and historical period surround his Second Empire world as a whole, and being an objective and detached Naturalist, he tended to approach his material in terms of a collective consciousness. Specifically, *Germinal* deals with collective misery, collective confrontation, and some vague promise of collective reform. In the Marxist interpretation of Darwin's law of natural selection, we somehow feel in *Germinal* that the absentee-owners of the Montsou mines will bring on their own ruin and that the system of "laissez-faire" capitalism which they so fervently embrace will, likewise, fall into a shambles. We feel, also, that in spite of Etienne Lantier's personal lack of success in leading the Montsou strike, there will be another day that will come and that it will bring an even bigger and better organized strike.

Zola suggested in *Germinal* that, despite the power of the military police and the seeming quiet that martial law brings, the ultimate power lies with the masses. The miners will literally spring from the earth: "la germination allait faire bientot eclater la terre" / "the germination would soon enough upturn the earth"; on the heels of misery will come a kind of salvation through socio-scientific consciousness, preceded by an inevitable cataclysm which will give way to a new system. The capitalist demagogue of *Germinal* is Emile Zola's economic counterpart to his biological "premiere lesion organique" / "primary organic lesion" of the other more primitive novels. As Doctor Pascal Rougon will elude and cure the hereditary bad seed of Zola's families as a kind of "Ubermensch," or Nietzschean "Superman," so too will future generations of miners be able to cure the disease of inhuman working conditions and labor exploitation by collective consciousness and organized power to the people.

ZOLA'S SYSTEMATIC THEORY OF NATURALISM

Despite the fact that many observers today might consider Zola's scientific theory of Naturalism to be ludicrously oversimplified, that it is really nothing more than an unresolved and subjective plan unapplicable to the novel on account of the fact that no one can "discover" something in a character that he has not already "planted" in the first place, Zola's theory serves well as a plan for the systematic demonstration of collective group patterns as manifest in the working-class novels of the Rougon-Macquart which include the proletarian masterpieces *L'Assommoir* (The Drinking Establishment), *Germinal, La Bete Humaine* (The Human Beast), and *La Terre* (The Earth).

LITERATURE TURNS TO SCIENCE

Because so many of the Romantics found only disillusionment in their quest through imagination and preconceived artistic selection for a better world in a period of such political ructions as the 1848 Revolution in France and the new political consciousness of democracy, many of the authors of the second half of the nineteenth century turned to the method of science. What seemed like a vague and poetic non-method of the lofty Romantics did not appear to be succeeding in implementing real change. By contrast to the idealism and lyricism of the Romantics and Sentimental Realists, the method of science seemed to be the key to attaining results. By the end of the nineteenth century, virtually every academic discipline was permeated with some sort of predilection with science, be it in some set of formulae or in a conspicuously scientifically-oriented vocabulary. In observing the success of the scientific method around them, authors likewise decided to adopt this method in their writing.

REALISM AND NATURALISM COMPARED

In its simplest and most original form, the system of Naturalism was merely an extension of **Realism** and a reaction to Romanticism. Realism, which was conceived to depict life as it actually was through a conscientious fidelity to nature, became extended into a precise system, a set of formulae involving objective and impartial modes of artistic selection supposedly excluding all of the subjective or preconceived modes of artistic selection revered by the Romantics. Zola's system of Naturalism dictated that fiction must follow the rigid methods of science, in being based solely on "human documents" provided by microscopic clinical observation of either the present, or the past retrospective observation through the scientific accumulation of research data. It was with these "human documents" provided by the author's present and the research data of his immediate past, that he assembled his celebrated preliminary sketches, or "ebauches," of his Rougon-Macquart novels. Considerable research has been executed within recent years on these "ebauches" by prominent scholars in attempting to scientifically and objectively reassemble Emile Zola's actual direct observations and experiences. The bulk of "ebauche" research has been conducted on the author's notes on news actualities utilized in *Germinal* concerning coal mine conditions and the circumstances surrounding the mining strikes of Aubin, Anzin, and La Ricamarie.

The most eminent research on these events of the 1860s appears in the works of Elliott M. Grant, Professor of French Emeritus of Williams College, Williamstown, Massachusetts. His research is of such outstanding quality that the editors of the authoritative annotated critical edition in French of the Rougon-Macquart, published by *Gallimard of Paris*, documented the five-volume set with acknowledged material from Professor Grant's extensive research. It is very much to the advantage of the American student that this considerable quantity of superlative research was written in the English language and is easily accessible in Grant's numerous journal articles and his two comprehensive books. The novel of Emile Zola which draws Elliott Grant's particular interest is *Germinal*, on which he has pursued considerable study. Professor Philip D. Walker of the University of California and the British scholar, F. W. J. Hemmings, have also conducted a considerable volume of top-level research on the Rougon-Macquart as a whole and *Germinal* as a self-contained work.

Zola postulated his theory of Naturalism in his Preface to *La Fortune des Rougons* (The Fortune of the Rougons) of 1871 and in his *Le Roman Experimental* (The Experimental Novel) of 1880. Influential to Zola's articulated theory were the extra-literary influences mentioned in the previous section as well as the pervasive atmosphere of revolution and scientific change that permeated Zola's France. France, as direct heir to the Enlightenment, bore a tremendous confidence in the potential of science and the rational faculties of man, and the influence of such ideas as Mendel's theory of dominant and recessive hereditary characteristics as well as Claude Bernard's methodology and hypotheses, permeate Emile Zola's Rougon-Macquart. Taine's theory of literature as demonstration of causal factors, as a kind of fictional cause-effect analysis of heredity, environment, and era is also predominant in the conception of Zola's works, as well as the scientifically, imbued mentalities of Darwin, Comte, and Marx.

ZOLAISM

In his Preface to *La Fortune des Rougons* (The Fortune of the Rougons) and *Le Roman Experimental* (The Experimental Novel),

Zola suggested that the novel, as the fictional counterpart of discursive cause-effect analysis, must set forth to reflect the process of research and observation in characters, setting, and epoch as in the clinical observation of specimens in a laboratory. Ideally, the method would be applied in an airtight, controlled environment so as to eliminate the risk of subjective contamination of the specimens by the author's imagination. Characters were to be conceived and put forth as fictional representatives in accordance with scientific aspects of sociology, psychology, and hereditary laws. They were to be, likewise, placed in a deterministic controlled environment representing given periods of time and factors of space, their conduct evolving causally from heredity, personality, environment, and historical period.

Consequently, the Naturalistic novel was to serve as a study of the genesis and growth of physical and psychological traits set in the context of a study of the social macrocosm of Zola's nineteenth-century France. The author's Naturalistic world became scientifically mechanistic and philosophically materialistic. Likewise, in its minute and microscopic portrayal of the world of phenomena, Zola's writing nearly abandoned the artistic selectivity of such prophetic Romantics as Victor Hugo (*Les Miserables* / *The Impoverished*) and the creatively selective Realist precursor of Naturalism, Gustave Flaubert (*Madame Bovary*).

In spite of the fact that Emile Zola scrupulously studied Claude Bernard's *Introduction a l'etude de la medicine* (Introduction to the Study of Medicine) and used it as an obvious model for *Le Roman Experimental* (The Experimental Novel), he was also one of many who tended to accept scientific determinism as the spirit of the times. He considered Naturalism, "scientisme" set to formula, as indigenous to French life in general, often referring to such earlier thinkers as the skeptic Montaigne and the deist Diderot as Naturalists.

THE NOVEL AS A LABORATORY REPORT

Emile Zola's *Le Roman Experimental* (The Experimental Novel) basically argued that an author might validly approach his characters as laboratory guinea pigs and that performing the equivalent of clinical tests on them would yield practical information about scientifically ascertained human weaknesses as root causes of misery and crime. An example of such human weakness which may be discovered by experimental research is the "premiere lesion organique" / "primary organic lesion" which may bring hereditary vice or weakness for generations upon generations in a family line. It may also miss certain descendants by genetic chance in accordance with Mendel's theory of genetic regression and dominance, making possible such fortunate descendants of Zola's families as Dr. Pascal Rougon.

Zola tended to think that, once examined and understood in scientific terms, the "organic lesion" could be cured on similar terms-through the wonders of scientific knowledge and medicine. With enough strenuous effort, human nature itself could be perfected. As oversimplistic as this may sound to the twentieth-century reader whose doubts as to the infallibility of science have been aroused by the temper of our own times, Zola's theory reveals an innocence and confidence which the nineteenth century still had for science. To this extent, Emile Zola was a product of his age, the post-Enlightenment. His presentation of contemporary history, the Second Empire, provided him with laboratory material for hypothesizing on humanity as a whole; he attempted to derive universally applicable laws from his "microcosm," which included samplings from the entire complex of urban-industrial society.

A MODERN EVE

From a moral standpoint, Zola's specimens of humanity have fallen into chaos by abandoning the old moral values and by creating a military-industrial "progress" - oriented society in which the absolute values of religion and metaphysics seem to no longer be operable. The curse of Eden mutates into the scientific and positivistic "organic lesion," with the Eve-figure becoming the alcoholically accursed Tante Dide, the ancestress of both the Rougon and Macquart families. She partakes of the forbidden brew rather than of the forbidden fruit, making the inevitable fall a scientific and hereditary one rather than a theological one.

Redemption, likewise, is along scientific lines in the hereditarily emancipated Dr. Pascal and his scientific mission. He has, in a sense, emerged from the adversities of heredity and environment to become Zola's medical "Übermensch" / "Superman," who in Nietzschean terms rises from the chaos and rubble of the old world. The working out of this family curse, in mythopoetic terms, reminds us somewhat of the Classical working out of the predetermined curse on the House of Atreus, as recorded in ancient myth and in Aeschylus's tragedy, *the Oresteia*. Blood relatives proliferate, bringing all sorts of violence upon one another as in the cases of the victimized Thyestes, the sacrilegious Agamemnon, the unfaithful and tyrannical Clytemnestra, the cowardly Aegisthus, and the ill-fated and yet emancipated Orestes. Dr. Pascal Rougon's liberation operates with the precision of "deus ex machina," bringing back vivid memories of the court of justice in *The Eumenides*, Aeschylus's final play in his deterministic and mythically powerful trilogy. Dr. Pascal, thus, becomes the savior-figure, serving the scientific and, as we are to discover in the twentieth century, very fallible godhead. An interested student could enlarge upon the doctor-figure in deterministic literature by examining Emile Zola's *Le Docteur Pascal* (Doctor Pascal) and Albert Camus' *La Peste* (The Plague), two novels presented in a highly objectified journalistic style but reflecting different periods in history.

WEAKNESS OF ZOLAISM

The fallacy of Zolaesque Naturalism lies in the fact that no writer of fiction (or of non-fiction, either) can be completely objective in the clinical sense; as is usually the case with rigid theories, the theory of Naturalism serves as a guide to method rather than existing as an infallible absolute. Consistent with Zola's theory, however, the Rougon-Macquart cycle sets out to trace the "natural and social history of a family under the Second Empire." Zola's cycle, in fact, was designed to vaguely supplement Honore Balzac's **epic** ninety-one novel-cycle, *La Comedie Humaine* (The Human Comedy), written during and depicting the early part of the nineteenth century. The Rougon-Macquart cycle exposes the full spectrum of the major trades and businesses of the late nineteenth century industrial and commercial bourgeois milieu: peasant farmer, laundress, coal miner, prostitute, railroad man, department-store retailmerchant, stockbroker, corporate director, revolutionary. The psycho-hereditary factors become evident particularly through the first and twentieth volumes of the cycle, *La Fortune des Rougons* and *Le Docteur Pascal*. The first lays the groundwork for the succeeding nineteen volumes; the last presents clinical case histories of individual family members rooted from the "premiere lesion organique" / "primary organic lesion" which functions as an individual as well as a collective neurotic driving force. Nevertheless as a creative inventor, Zola at times reached an artistic stature which anticipated our own Nobel Prize winner and literary giant of Naturalism, John Steinbeck. The American author, under the influence of Emile Zola, was to make the flights and introspections of the fugitive hero amid economic, environmental, and hereditary adversity an indispensable staple in U. S. fiction.

It seems, in a way, that what Zola theorized in *Le Roman Experimental* (The Experimental Novel) and what he actually practiced in his Rougon-Macquart, especially in *Germinal*, were two different things. He theorized that a novelist was a scientific observer and an experimenter, contributing to humanity by effecting scientific discoveries on fictional but true-to-life people. Major questions which one may ask, however, are those inquiries which one might make as to how a novelist can possibly discover heretofore unknown elements in characters which he himself has created, and related inquiries probing the possibility that these discoveries are actually data planted by the author who knew ahead of time as to how his novels were determined to progress. Zola had also theorized that the perfectly conceived objective Naturalistic fictional plot would just grow logically and automatically, by inherent natural laws, out of the author's uncontaminated scientific observations. Zola believed, from a theoretical standpoint, that the "ebauches" would naturally grow into vast novels on a completely impartial, neutral, and scientific basis.

The fact of the matter was that Emile Zola's novels did grow naturally from the "ebauches," but they grew along monumental mythic and poetic lines as well as along scientific lines. While Zola postulated his vast scientific theories, he also let fall from his hand statements alluding to the idea that fiction was, in fact, a creative process as well as a scientific one. While this might appear to irrevocably contradict the theories, it made his best working-class novels the masterpieces of **epic** poetry and archetypal myth that they are. The analytical commentaries on *Germinal* deal primarily with Zola's application of creativity to his novel, his Naturalistic technique as blended with certain basic and profoundly pervasive modes of artistic selection.

ZOLA'S ACTUAL ESTHETIC

Specific remarks dropped by Emile Zola which seem to contradict his theories as set forth in *La Fortune des Rougons* and *Le Roman Experimental* are those brief but preeminent statements in which he alluded to "temperament" and his conception of a metaphorical "lie." Zola defined art as "a segment of nature seen through a temperament," remarking on the subject of temperament as early as his Preface to *Therese Raquin* of 1867. This type of definition of art concedes subjective forces in the process of creation, even Naturalistic creation, regardless of how apparently scientific a breakdown of temperament may be. More specifically, Zola conceded that creation is metaphorical, some profoundly truthful sort of "lie," embodying in the Naturalistic spectacle a deeply imaginative mythopoetic spectacle. In his famous letter to Henri Ceard, one of the younger writers of his Medan Circle, of March 22, 1885, Zola articulated a startlingly Proustian conception of **metaphor** or artistic vision. His "lie" would bring us to "a more complete understanding of the truth" which would ascend at "but a single beat of the wing straight to the realm of symbol." In the actual application of Zola's theories to literature, it was these comments on "temperament" and the metaphorical "lie" that, in truth, eclipsed all of the erudite scientific essays in the Le Roman Experimental collection. Despite the fact that the author thought a plot would just naturally grow from the actualities recorded in his "ebauches," his plots, in fact, grew from his own mythic consciousness. The journal data would merely serve as specific contemporary material, designed to elaborate upon the monumental archetypal plan underlying the particular story.

NATURALISM AS A LITERARY FORCE

While it is difficult to chronologically delineate the turn from Realism to Naturalism, it is clear that the scientific and sociological emphases of the period from 1870 onward certainly eclipsed the artistic and selective emphases of earlier Romantic and Sentimental Realist writing, thus heralding the Naturalistic spirit to the literature of France and Germany. It was only with the unseating of Naturalism by Expressionism that the peak of Naturalism was obscured in the years immediately preceding and surrounding World War I, but as a literary force, Naturalism is still prominent today. Zola's literature, especially the masterpiece *Germinal*, marks the bridge between the two major phases of Naturalism, pre-Expressionist and post-Expressionist, and draws upon the assets of both. Emile Zola had absorbed from nineteenth-century scientific luminaries the elements of hereditary, environment, and epoch as forces in his work bearing the preeminent characteristics of pre-World War I literary Naturalism, and the author also absorbed some of the radical aspects of the new phase of Naturalism as well, the phase of Expressionist nightmare and nascent Marxism.

Zola served his doctrine of scientific impartiality well as a basic method, not allowing himself to sink into the Marxist morass of propaganda into which many of the World War I authors fell. As well as being conscious of ineluctable biological forces which would appear to control human existence, he was also aware of the political and economic forces, forces which were to in influence most of the novels written between World War I and World War II. As well as touching the periphery of Expressionism, Zola infused the artistically selective and yet scientifically objective spirit of Impressionism into his novels. This served to extend Zola's Naturalism beyond its rigidly scientific beginnings, and provides the nucleus for subsequent sections of this volume as well as of the analytical commentaries on *Germinal*.

From a theoretical standpoint, the concept of Naturalism implies its characteristics, of which the primary ones in Zola's time were verisimilitude of language (*L'Assommoir* / The Drinking Establishment), leading ultimately to dialect and profanity in twentieth-century fiction; relative formlessness or vastness, corresponding to the formlessness and vastness of actual life; a turn toward the oppressed proletariat and away from the bourgeoisie of Balzac and Flaubert; a lack of faith in the individual's ability to control his destiny; and, usually an implied faith in some socio-political panacea. Most Naturalistic works are tragic without being actual tragedies in the Classical sense, for the sufferers are invariably the victims of forces beyond their control, and their suffering seems both needless and meaningless.

NATURALISM, REALISM, AND IMPRESSIONISM

It was the school of Realists who were basically the precursors to the Naturalists, and the essential distinction between **Realism** and Naturalism is one primarily of degree rather than of kind. The Naturalists theorized systematic formulae and presented generally harsher slices of life in their works, their basic credo being basically to unveil impartially the world as it actually exists.

FLAUBERT AND ZOLA

Of monumental significance in Emile Zola's formulation of his dictum of impartiality, however, was one particular French Realist, his close friend Gustave Flaubert. The Realists tended to be fastidiously concerned with exactitude and Flaubert, their mentor, developed a highly perfect and specialized technique of revision by which he ground and honed his works to consummate compression by painstaking word-selection in the "le mot juste" / "the right word" technique. Unlike Flaubert, Zola seldom revised his prose, writing and publishing in wholesale volume as some huge automatic machine. From Flaubert, however, Zola absorbed the nascent method of impartiality which the Realist writer had executed to near perfection in Madame Bovary, the ending of which leaves the reader with his own moral and philosophical conclusions to draw. The author himself hovered in the neutral corners, but he gave the reader to deduce generally pessimistic conclusions. Another Realist who was a master of this technique of complete impartiality was one of the younger writers of Zola's discipleship of the celebrated Medan Circle, the master of the bitterly pessimistic, objectively conceived short story, *Guy de Maupassant*. The Medan Circle, under Emile Zola's leadership, published a set of short stories relating to the Franco-Prussian War, *Les Soirees de Medan*, in 1880, in which Guy de Maupassant's masterpiece "Bel Ami" appeared.

Among the other French Realists influential upon Emile Zola were Honore Balzac and the fastidious pseudo-Naturalists, Edmond and Jules de Goncourt. Balzac's *La Comedie Humaine* (The Human Comedy) embodied in a fictional colossus a treatment of the first half of the nineteenth century that inspired Zola to embody the second half into his own fictional colossus. Balzac's ninety-one novel set served to establish a model for

Zola's twenty-novel set. While the Realist Balzac constructed scores of individualized characters, the Naturalist Zola was to gain from Flaubert a mastery of crowds and collective representative groups. The contribution to Zola of Edmond and Jules de Goncourt was *Germinie Lacerteux*, the first French novel dealing in a vaguely scientific way with a protagonist's fall into low life.

The Romantic pre-Realist, Victor Hugo, was to be of profound influence upon Zola even though he criticized Hugo's style. Hugo's mark is highly conspicuous in Zola's early works, and a subtle infusion of that brand of artistic selection and lyrical poetic imagination is evident in works as late as *Germinal*. Many believe that the Zola of Romantic-Realist inspiration is the Zola that became a master. Zola's adversaries, which were to include the eminent French critic, Ferdinand Brunetiere, and the five younger writers who were to compose "The Manifesto of the Five," considered his theory and technique of Naturalism to be virtually bankrupt and totally used up.

ZOLA, TURGENEV, AND JAMES

Outside of France, Emile Zola received a great deal of Realist influence from such Russian Realists as Ivan Turgenev. Channels of literary exchange were wide open between France and Russia, Zola's works being often translated in Russian publications, and Russian works likewise gaining exposure in France. Among the Russian Realists to influence Zola were Tolstoi and, more particularly Turgenev, whose demagogues appear in such new guises in Zola's work as that of the anarchist Souvarine in *Germinal*.

Finally, Emile Zola was to himself influence Realists outside of France as well. Among the Zola-influenced Realists of England were George Moore, and more significantly, the English master, Henry James. James not only praised Emile Zola's work, but in the tradition of Zola, created his own theory of fiction.

NATURALISM AND IMPRESSIONIST PAINTING

By the end of the nineteenth century, painting had become a preeminent art form in France. The Impressionists had formally announced their "school" in 1874, and, in a sense, emerged as counterparts in painting to the Naturalists in literature. Like the Naturalistic writers, the Impressionistic painters were bolder, more unorthodox, and more scientifically oriented than the Realists. Beginning as disciples of Courbet, such painters as Manet, Whistler, Pissarro, Cezanne, and others became daring and innovative experimenters in technique and subject matter. They often used nature as the subject of their paintings, using strong colors, and depicting ordinary everyday people instead of neo-Classical models. Often the Impressionists were scathed by critics for what appeared to be unpainstaking technique in the eyes of more orthodox viewers.

More specifically, what Naturalism and Impressionism have in common, even though many scholars do not associate the two together, is a basic scientifically-oriented method as applied to some form of art. One associates Naturalism with the art of the novel, and one associates Impressionism with the art of the canvas; but they are both theoretically conceived in detachment and are directed toward objective "innocent eye" interpretation.

While the novelist applying the theory of Naturalism would pursue his work in terms of the natural laws of heredity, environment, and historical period-or, more specifically, of society, politics, and economics-the painter applying the precepts of Impressionism would pursue his work in terms of the natural laws of color. In terms of science, color operates in constructs of additive, subtractive, and complementary primaries. The Impressionists painted with the objective vision of "scientisme," through the objective application of strategically adjacent primary colors on the canvas. These primaries include the reds, the blues, and sometimes the greens or the yellows. In terms of the laws of optics, spectral reactions suggestive of other colors may be created through interactions of the primaries-yielding intermediate colors, such as purple with adjacent red and blue, or black through subtractive interaction, or white through additive interaction.

Naturalism and Impressionism are both extensions of **Realism** because they set the ideals of **Realism** to coherent scientifically oriented systems. While the Realist novelists and painters fastidiously strove to portray life as it actually is, they had no formula or systematic method on which to turn to assure them that they were not contaminating their supposedly objective experimental work with imaginative elements. Consistent with this spirit, the painting of the Impressionists is ideally viewed from a slight distance. Emile Zola, himself, identified Naturalism and Impressionism with one another, for he was highly conscious of the Positivistic and experimental spirit inherent to both.

INTRODUCTION TO EMILE ZOLA

. . . .

1840

Emile Edouard Charles Antoine Zola born in the wholesale market district of Paris, about which he was to write in *Le Ventre de Paris* (The Paris Marketplace). His father, Francesco Zola, was a foreigner to France, an Italian civil engineer from Venice of Greek and Italian heritage, who had left Italy during the time following the fall of Napoleon when Austrian oppression became insufferable to him. His mother, Emilie Aubert (Zola), was of relentlessly proud French upper-peasant stock. Emile was the only child in the family, born just a year after the marriage of his parents.

1840

P. J. Proudhon (to whose ideology Marx was basically opposed) published *Qu'est-ce que la propriete?* (What is Property?). Within this decade, Paris was to become a primary place of ferment for Marxism.

1840

Auguste Comte completed his first major treatise, begun in 1830, *Course of Positivist Philosophy*. Positivism was to dominate French intellectual activity during the Second Empire.

1842

The Zola family returned to Aix-en-Provence where Zola's father had been for years investigating the possibilities for, and drawing up plans for, building a water canal for this parched southern city. Regarding these canal plans many specifics are obscure, but numerous apparently unfounded suspicious remarks alluding to "schemes," appear in several Zola biographies. Ernest Vizetelly, the son of Henry Vizetelly, Zola's contemporary English translator-publisher, defends Zola's father admirably and adamantly in a thorough early biography.

1844

Marx emigrated from Germany to France to become acquainted with French Socialist writers, establishing a friendship with Friedrich Engels. The influences therefrom led Marx to become a Socialist and to publish the *Communist Manifesto* with Engels four years later.

1847

Zola's father died suddenly at Marseilles at the age of 51, thus marking the beginning of straitened financial conditions for Zola's mother who, nevertheless, desired that her son secure formal education. The memory of Aix-en-Provence (his fictional *Plassans*) is to be endearing with respect to its open countryside; but it is to be bitter with regard to the fact that his father's financial status had been adversely affected by a power shift in French government and unanticipated decision changes regarding funding. Some suggest, especially Angus Wilson, that Zola's mother was competitive and domineering for her son's devotion, eclipsing the father figure in the writer's life. This premise seems to be well substantiated by the profusion of Emilie-Aubert-Zola-figures which appear, under various guises, in the novels. A subsequent triangular marital conflict syndrome is also ominously manifest as a basic Zola **theme** in *La Joie de Vivre* (The Joy of Living) in his handling of Mme. Chanteau and her son Lazare, and in *Le Docteur Pascal* (Doctor Pascal) in his handling of Felicite Rougon.

1847

From his exile in Brussels, Marx wrote a terse reply to Proudhon's book, *Philosophie de la Misere* (Philosophy of Poverty), calling it *Misere de la Philosophie* (Poverty of Philosophy) in which Marx developed his basic economic interpretation of history, pitting his search for the inevitable, which would result from historical forces, against Proudhon's (and the utopian socialists') search for a moral social order.

1848

On the eve of the French February Revolution, Marx and Engels published the *Communist Manifesto*, written as a platform for the Communist league. The *Manifesto* was well timed, appearing when revolution was in the air.

1848

Second Republic: February Revolution: Attempts to organize labor end in the massacres of the "June Days." The year 1848 was a turning point in history for all of Europe, with irrevocable forces of revolution and change being set in motion.

1850

Marx published his Die Klassenkampfe in Frankreich 1848 bis 1850 (1850/1859), The Class Struggle in France from 1848 to 1850, applying his philosophy of history to the French civil warfare between workers and middle class.

1850

Dr. Lucas, all but forgotten today, published the *Traite Philosophique et physiologique de l'heredite naturelle* (The Philosophical and Physiological Treatise of Natural Heredity) which was to be instrumental in the formation of Zola's Naturalistic theory of heredity. Lucas became Zola's model for his Dr. Pascal Rougon in *Le Docteur Pascal*.

1851

The "coup d' etat" of Louis Napoleon (Napoleon III), was to bring a spirit of revolution and reaction. Zola's mother's hopes for funds from Thiers, drawn from his father's interests, vanish, thus forcing her to move to progressively poorer dwellings to provide educational funds for her son.

1851

Exhibition of the Crystal Palace in London, embodying the tone of the times, celebrated as a superlative feat of progress, but also symbolic of the ascending bourgeoisie and the domination of the world by mechanized industry. Ironically, it was to fall into flaming molten ruins in 1936.

1852

Second Empire.

1853

Zola's early friendship with Paul Cezanne began at Aix College, where he accumulated much of his Classical education and read the French Romantics.

1854

Comte published the fourth and final volume of his *System of Positive Polity*, begun in 1851.

1857

Zola's maternal grandmother died, with whom Zola's mother lived during these years of financial hardship. Zola's mother returned to Paris from Aix feeling that she could better supervise her interests (which were never made clear to her) in the canal business.

1857

Flaubert's Madame Bovary published.

1858

Zola joined his mother in Paris, transferring from Aix College to the Lycee and Saint-Louis.

1859

Darwin published *On the Origin of Species by Natural Selection*, marking a basic shift in educational curricula in years to come from the Classics to science, the Second Empire being dominated by Positivism and "Scientisme." When Darwin was translated into French, Zola read his work voraciously.

1859-60

After failing his baccalaureate, Zola lived in dire poverty, feeling himself to be a total failure to his mother. Much has been reported by biographers on this phase of the author's life during which he worked on the Paris docks.

1862

Zola was hired by the *Hachette* publishing house as a sales clerk, but eventually became publicity chief, thereby developing a shrewd eye for press strategy and salable books. He was to become the first French author to literally sell in the hundreds of thousands; at this time, however, he was making his first celebrated acquaintances, among them, Hippolyte Taine, the apostle of hereditary and environmental influence.

1862

Zola naturalized as a French citizen because his father had been an immigrant.

1863:

After being cautioned by *Hachette* as to the poor salability of poetry, Zola wrote his first prose for publication: short stories upon the manager's advice.

1864

Clemence Royer translated Darwin into French. Dr. Letourneau published *Physiologie des Passions*. Both were read enthusiastically by Zola.

1864

The First Workingmen's Association was founded in London out of a meeting organized by Marx. Despite the fact that Zola was not politically engage at this point in his life, he was interested in the Party and well-read regarding its activities. The Zola who had known urban poverty in Paris was a very different person from the sheltered boy of Aix.

During the summer and fall of 1864, Zola met Gabrielle-Eleonore-Alexandrine Meley, apparently through his friendship with Cezanne, but Zola's mother disapproved of her.

Lacroix published Zola's first book, the *Contes a Ninon* (Stories to Ninon).

1865

Edmond and Jules Goncourt published *Germinie Lacerteux*, the first celebrated French novel dealing with the deprivations of the lower classes in a basically Naturalistic technique. Zola and the Goncourt brothers were friends and their influence upon him is unmistakable.

Zola set out as a literary critic in such publications as *Salut Public* and *Petit Journal*.

Claude Bernard published his *Introduction a l'etude de la medicine experimentale* (Introduction to the Study of Experimental Medicine) around which Zola based part of his Naturalistic technique and most of *Le Roman Experimental* (The Experimental Novel).

1866

Zola published the grim novel *La Confession de Claude* (The Confession of Claude) which prompted Hachette to warn Zola to write only on the manager's terms as the novel had raised a scandal and drawn the attentions of the police Procureur Imperial. Not being able to write on controversial subjects,

Zola decided to leave the publisher altogether now that he was writing marketable material.

Zola became a litterateur for *L'Evenement*, a new journal begun by the shrewd publisher Villemessant.

Zola championed the art of the controversial Impressionists, especially that of Edouard Manet, who was to subsequently become Zola's friend, in the newspaper *Figaro* and in *L'Evenement*. Zola raised a furor regarding the aesthetic values of the new school of painters.

Zola presented two definitions of the novel in written communication to the *Congres Scientifique of Aix*.

1867

Zola published a biographical and critical study of Manet, to whose bold new art he was devoted.

Zola's scientific theories were first put into practice in Therese Raquin, which was first announced in *La Bibliographie de la France*. The first edition bore the famous quotation of Hippolyte Taine: "Le vice et la vertu, qui sont des produits comme le vitriol et le sucre," / "Vice and virtue, which are products like vinegar and sugar," later to be deleted upon consultation with Sainte-Beuve.

Marx published the beginnings of *Das Kapital* (Capital), volumes of which were to subsequently appear in 1885 and 1894. The treatise basically develops a theory of the capitalist system, emphasizing its dynamism and capacity for self-destruction.

1868

After Zola's authorization to found a journal was suppressed, several opposition journals filled with invective against him appeared. From 1868–1870 he made notable contributions to the *Tribune*, *Rappel*, *La Cloche*, and *Gaulois*.

Madeleine Ferat, Zola's second scientific novel, was published. It was at the end of 1868 that he first mentioned an embryonic project, a projected collection of ten volumes consisting of a vast novel about a family.

1869

During this time, near the end of the Second Empire, Zola wrote resumes of numerous bloody coal-mine strikes taking place at Aubin and La Ricamarie, in the northern part of France. These resumes, plus his own impressions of the strikes, provided much of the background and plot material contained in the "ebauches" of *Germinal*.

1868–1670

During these years, Zola worked on the "ebauches" for the first three Rougon-Macquart novels.

1869

Flaubert's *L'Education Sentimentale* published.

1870

The Third Republic was proclaimed after the humiliating defeat of Napoleon in the Franco-Prussian War, after which dissension over what were considered to be overly compromising peace terms to Prussia brought siege and civil war to Paris. Zola married Gabrielle-Alexandrine Meley and went south to engage in local Republican politics.

A journal, moderately opposed to Zola, began to publish the Rougon-Macquart novels in serial form.

1870

Zola wrote a controversial article for *La Cloche*, "Vive la France," attacking certain laws and elements of government. It bore the same liberal tone as his later "J'Accuse," and seems to have been written by the same defiant hand.

La Fortune des Rougon, the first novel of the Rougon-Macquart, appeared in a full library edition, receiving the compliments of Gustave Flaubert. The first six novels of the cycle came out at the rate of one per year from 1881–1886; the rest came out between 1878–1893.

1871

After seeking a position in the local Republican administration of Bordeaux, Zola was to become correspondent to the National Assembly of Bordeaux and Versailles for *La Cloche* and *Semaphore de Marseille*. And, as *Le Siecle* was picking up the temporarily tabled serialization of the Rougon-Macquart, the Paris Commune was beginning to operate at Montmartre. The Paris Commune, which extended from March 18 to May 23, was to be followed by a week of infamy, the "semaine sanglante" or "bloody week," in which 20,000 persons were slain in the promptly quelled Paris uprising. Zola did not participate in the Franco-Prussian War or remain in Paris immediately thereafter because he had his wife and mother as dependents.

1872

Zola served as parliamentarian chronicler for *La Cloche*. *La Curee* (The Plunder) officially released as the second volume of the Rougon-Macquart.

1873

With the financial failure of publisher Lacroix, publisher Charpentier released *La Ventre de Paris* (The Paris Marketplace) as the third volume of the twenty-volume set.

La Conquete de Plassans (Plassans Conquered), the fourth novel, was published in serialized form by *Le Siecle*.

1874

The Nouveaux Contes a Ninon (New Ninon Stories) were published.

The Impressionist Movement finally began as a school, with an official and very controversial exhibition of paintings.

1875

Zola began an association with the Russian journal, *Messager de l'Europe*, of Saint Petersburg, which consisted of the publication of some sixty-four articles up until December of 1880.

The fifth novel of the Rougon-Macquart, *La Faute de l'Abbe Mouret* (The Abbe Mouret's Mistake), was published in translation in *Messager de l'Europe*, interesting evidence of the strong bind between French and Russian literary interests.

1876

The sixth novel, *Son Excellence Eugene Rougon* (His Excellency, Eugene Rougon), also appeared in *Messager d l'Europe*.

Menier's journal, *Le Bien Public*, began *L'Assommoir* (The Drinking Establishment) in serialized form, but dropped it within two months. After *Le Republique des Lettres* assumed it, Zola became instantaneously famous.

1877

The official library volume of *L'Assommoir* was released as the seventh novel of the Rougon-Macquart.

1878

Zola bought his famous house at Medan with money earned from *L'Assommoir* royalties.

As well as publishing *Un Page d'Amour* (A Leaf of Love) as volume eight of the cycle, Zola decided to publish his definitive Rougon-Macquart family genealogy.

Zola read the 1865 work by Claude Bernard, using it as a model in *Le Roman Experimental* (The Experimental Novel).

1879

Henrik Ibsen's Naturalistic masterpiece, "A Doll's House," presented on the stage.

1880

Charpentier published *Nana*, the ninth volume of the Rougon-Macquart, with huge sales.

The famous set of short stories, *Les Soirees de Medan*, appeared as exemplifying the Naturalistic school.

Gustave Flaubert died suddenly at Croisset. The loss of his best friend grieved Zola and the effect of it may be seen in his work.

Zola wrote a series of articles for *Le Figaro* for a year, of which most appear in the 1881 publication, *Une Compagne*.

Zola's mother died on October 17-a traumatic experience for the author from which he recovered only gradually, but which spawned some of the masterpieces of enormity and grimness which are celebrated as his best work.

In publishing *Le Roman Experimental* (The Experimental Novel), in which he declared his Naturalism, he attempted to set his half-completed Rougon-Macquart to a scientifically rationalized formula in the manner of Claude Bernard.

Henrik Ibsen's "Ghosts" was presented, creating a shock reaction with its hereditary **theme**. Some of Zola's novels were to cause similar shock reactions.

1881

The stopping of payments by La Banque l'Union Generale was a major historical event of the Third Republic, providing a large amount of material for two major later works of literature: Guy de Maupassant's "Bel Ami" and Emile Zola's *L'Argent* (Money). Zola published the tenth Rougon-Macquart novel, *Pot-Bouille* (The Stew Kettle), which served as the perfect bourgeois-oriented counterpart to the slum story, *L'Assommoir* (The Drinking Establishment).

1883

Zola published the eleventh novel of the set, *Au Bonheur des Dames* (Feminine Fancies), a story of retail merchandising.

1884

Zola published the twelfth novel in an extremely bitter frame of mind, giving a deliberate ironic twist to the title, *La Joie de Vivre* (The Joy of Living). Contributing factors to Zola's pathological morbidity at this time included the recent death of his mother, memories of hostilities between her and his wife, his childlessness, and the recent death of Gustave Flaubert.

Friedrich Nietzsche published *Also Sprach Zarathustra* (Thus Spoke Zarathustra).

Henry Vizetelly's efforts with Zola translations began, *L'Assommoir* appearing in the English language the following year.

Coal mine strikes broke out in Northern France and Belgium.

1885

Most critics today agree that publication of the library edition of the thirteenth novel of the Rougon-Macquart, a story about a coal mine strike in Northern France entitled *Germinal*, marked the pinnacle of Zola's genius.

Victor Hugo, a novelist admired by Zola since his early days, died.

1886

Zola published the fourteenth novel, *L'Oeuvre* (The Work of Art), vaguely based on the author's friendship with Cezanne.

Nietzsche published *Jenseits von Gut und Bose* (Beyond Good and Evil).

1887

Le Figaro published "The Manifesto of the Five," the manifesto of five young writers who turned against Zola's technique in general and against *La Terre* (The Earth) in particular. By this time, Naturalism was receding in influence with the appearance of such writers as Huysmans, Verlaine, Mallarme, and other Symbolists. After publication of *La Terre* (The Earth) as the fifteenth novel of the cycle, the Goncourt brothers published their *Journal*.

1888

Zola met with Jeanne-Sophie Adele Rozerot at Medan. With his emergence from psychic depression, Zola's writing began to atrophy and lose its sense of magnitude and scale.

Sixteenth novel, *La Reve* (The Vision), published.

Henry Vizetelly's ill-fated English translation of *La Terre* as *Soil* was published, causing a furor in England.

1889

Birth of Denise, Zola's daughter by Jeanne Rozerot.

Seventeenth novel of the cycle, *La Bete Humaine* (The Human Beast), a novel about working men on the railroads, published. It is considered, along with *L'Assommoir*, *Germinal*, and *La Terre*, to be one of Zola's outstanding working-class novels.

1890

Ibsen's "Hedda Gabler" presented.

1891

Eighteenth novel of the cycle, *L'Argent* (Money), about the world of high finance, published.

Birth of Jacques, Zola's son by Jeanne Rozerot.

1892

Nineteenth novel, *La Debacle* (The Debacle), dealing with the disastrous Franco-Prussian War, published.

1893

Le Docteur Pascal (Doctor Pascal), the twentieth novel, published.

1894

Lourdes, the first novel of a set entitled *Trois Villes* (Three Cities), published.

Captain Alfred Dreyfus condemned for treason on what has since been considered to be circumstantial evidence.

1895

Havelock Ellis, eminent and controversial English psychologist, published an English translation of *Germinal*.

1896

Rome, the second novel of *Trois Villes*, published.

1897

Le Figaro published an article by Zola on the Dreyfus Affair.

1898

L'Aurore published the celebrated letter, "J'Accuse."

Paris, the third novel of *Trois Villes*, published.

In reaction to "J'Accuse," Zola was forced into exile into England, where he stayed for some months with the Vizetellys, his closest English friends.

1899

Zola returned to France after a petition had been circulated by Marcel Proust on Zola's behalf, at the urging of Anatole France.

Fecondite (Fecundity), the first of the *Quatre Evangiles* (Four Gospels), published.

1901

Travail, the second work of the set, published.

1902

Zola's presumably accidental death by carbon monoxide asphyxiation in Paris on September 29.

Verite, the third work of *Quatre Evangiles*, was published the following year, but *Justice* never passed the planning stage.

1928-9

The first critical edition of the Rougon-Macquart published by Maurice Le Blond, Zola's son-in-law.

1960-7

Bibliotheque de la Pleiade edition of the Rougon-Macquart, published in five critically annotated volumes, by A. Lanoux and H. Mitterand.

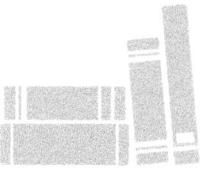

GERMINAL

. . . .

IMPRESSIONISM AND "GERMINAL"

Among the causes which Emile Zola courageously championed, under the risk of his own reputation and success, was that of the Impressionists. To the consternation of many well-established art critics and journal publishers, Emile Zola defended the subject matter, color technique, and artistic conception of Edouard Manet's controversial Impressionistic art. Even the term "Impressionism" was originally one of critical ridicule and disdain. Impressionism, however, ultimately was to have a profound effect upon *Germinal*, and large sections of analytical commentaries on the novel concern themselves with this subject.

Emile Zola had numerous artist friends, among them Paul Cezanne, who was his closest school friend at the College d'Aix at Aix-en-Provence in his early days. Cezanne eventually became celebrated as the forerunner of the twentieth-century school of Cubism, and if one examines closely Zola's description of the fruit in Les Halles in *Le Ventre de Paris* (The Paris Marketplace), one can sense the extraordinary volume and spatial dimension amid giant masses of primary Impressionistic color in the book. Zola's *L'Oeuvre* (The Work of Art), another one of the Rougon-Macquart novels, concerns itself with the life of Cezanne. The celebrated painter broke off his friendship with Zola at about this time as he did with nearly everyone he knew.

Edouard Manet, whom Zola so ardently defended, became the author's friend and painted his portrait. He influenced Zola's artistic vision through his awareness of everyday commonplaces from low life as potential and powerful artistic subject matter. Like Manet, Zola artistically was to create natural landscapes, simple houses, and ordinary people such as peddlers and urchins.

As well as adopting the basic subject-matter of the Impressionists, Zola also adopted literary counterparts of such techniques as the impasto brush stroke effect in large color areas. Likewise, he was often to be concerned with Impressionistic weather effects, utilizing such techniques as chiaroscuro and sfumato in setting them against the dark backdrop of *Germinal*.

INTRODUCTION TO THE "ROUGON-MACQUART" AND TO "GERMINAL"

Basically, the plot material of the Rougon-Macquart novels sporadically parallels the succession of events encompassing the Second Empire in France from the "coup d'etat" to its fall at Sedan in the Franco-Prussian catastrophe of 1870, recorded in *La Debacle* (The Debacle). Specifically, the Rougon-Macquart is the "natural and social history of a family under the Second Empire." The scientific and social-political ramifications of the cycle, in the context of Zola's Naturalistic theory, have already been discussed.

Attempts at summarizing each novel of the cycle are usually quite meaningless, but one may find brief correlated summaries of the Rougon-Macquart in Martin Turnell's *The Art of French Fiction*, and longer more comprehensive summaries in Elliott M. Grant's Emile Zola. Zola's enormous twenty-novel "roman fleuve," or "river novel," is a diversified fictional manifesto-a literary conglomerate condemning urban and industrial exploitation in documented, yet imaginative prose. Consistent with the Zolaesque predilection for the clinician's microscope is a kind of inherent and naturally consistent pulse-like oscillation between the Rougon-Macquart's violently potent novels and its gently passive ones. The violent novels include the working class masterpieces like *Germinal* and *La Terre*; the tranquil ones include the bourgeois novels like *L'Argent*. The most striking pulsation, however, exists at the **climax** of the set-between the ructions of *La Debacle* and the resolution of *Le Docteur Pascal*.

GROWING INTEREST IN "GERMINAL"

It was only a few years ago that the reader of Emile Zola tended to focus his studies of the Rougon-Macquart cycle on either *L'Assommoir* (The Drinking Establishment) or *Nana*. Many of the novels of the twenty-volume set are not commonly read at all, and *Germinal* itself remained relatively untouched by readers and commentators, especially in the United States, until very recently. While many critics have found *L'Assommoir* and *Nana* morally controversial, *Germinal* may have been more thoroughly avoided because of its Marxist overtones.

Several European critics, however, suggested a long time ago that *Germinal* was Zola's finest novel and that it was the undisputed mother lode of the Rougon-Macquart cycle. These critics included the controversial English psychologist, Havelock

Ellis, who translated *Germinal* into English, and the eminent French novelist, Andre Gide, who declared that the thirteenth Rougon-Macquart novel was one of the ten greatest novels ever written.

Today, contemporary modern critics of Emile Zola Like Elliott M. Grant fully acknowledge the supremacy of *Germinal* over the rest of Zola's work. In recent bibliographies, one can readily notice that the majority of new articles and books dealing with any aspect of Zola's Rougon-Macquart deal particularly with *Germinal* and generally with such radically modernist aspects of the work as its Expressionist and apocalyptic overtones. Articles have also been written concerning themselves with labor-management relations and Marxism in *Germinal*. One of the most striking aspects of the body of *Germinal* research is its degree of recency; most of the outstanding books and articles focusing on the mine novel have appeared during and since the 1960s.

ZOLA'S SOURCE MATERIALS

The strike in *Germinal* is based on actual strikes which Emile Zola observed during the 1860s at such places as Aubin and La Ricamarie in the northern coal-mining districts of France. Zola had gathered much of the data for his novel in the 1860s but delayed writing and publishing these other working-class novels because of oppressive censorship of material sympathetic to labor in the period following the Paris Commune. After the Paris uprising of 1871, novelists avoided writing on labor-management affairs. Related to this was the outlawing of membership to the International Workingmen's Association in 1872. By 1879, however, the Communards were amnestied and the workers formed their own party in 1880.

Zola started work on *Germinal* as a self-contained novel in 1884, but had much of the "ebauche" material assembled previously in his journal from the strike years. During this time Zola studied Marxism as well as its policy-making body, the International Workingmen's Association (First International). He inspected mines, interviewed mine workers, and gathered information on their political persuasions. Influential during this period was the thinking of Jules Guesde, a militant French Marxist and originally a follower of Mikhail Bakunin, the Russian anarchist who struggled with Marx for control of the International. In *Germinal*, we see the Guesdist in Pluchart and the Bakuninite in Souvarine, representative types of radical left-wing revolutionaries. Emile Zola kept scrupulous notes on the internal developments of the International and brought references to the London-headquartered institution into *Germinal*.

"GERMINAL" AS A "BILDUNGSROMAN"

Some might refer to *Germinal* as a "Bildungsroman" because it basically presents the self education and growth of a worker, Etienne Lantier, who at first has only vague and fragmentary knowledge of revolutionary theory, but who nevertheless inspires the confidence of the Maheu family, with whom he has been invited to lodge. Gradually, Lantier's knowledge of working conditions in the mines grows and, despite his lack of educated method or academic discipline in his assimilation and synthesis of theory, he begins to win the support of the Montsou workers as their leader, reaching his peak of triumph in the moonlit forest where he realizes his powers as an orator. Unaware that his supposed model Pluchart seems to know ahead of time that the strike will fail, Lantier optimistically leads his following on a march but unexpectedly loses control over the crowd. Pluchart, the Secretary of the Northern Federation of the International Workingmen's Association, seems to regard the miners' inevitably unsuccessful strike as but one early phase in a long series of phases of which the ultimate aim will be, in absorbing the miners into the International so that, one day, there will be a united revolution on an international scale. Etienne's tragedy is that he is so unread in the actual ways of revolution and so unaware of the extensive violence that it brings that he thinks but one work stoppage will force management to negotiate on the workers' terms regarding the pay scale. Little does he seem to realize, also, that a period of economic recession is the poorest time to decide to strike, and that the managers might well actually welcome work stoppage to cut overhead, cut supplies, and eventually raise prices. Some suggest that management would often provoke strike for this precise purpose.

Emile Zola's conception and execution of the *Germinal* plot chronologically parallel the influx and development of Socialism in France. German and French Marxism had their beginnings during and after the 1848 Revolutions, but elements of even more radical political unrest penetrated France from such places as Russia, where in 1861, Czar Alexander I was assassinated. When Zola was collecting his "ebauche" material for *Germinal*, an influential event took place in 1864. This was the enactment of the "law on coalitions," which rendered labor virtually powerless in matters of protest, allowing workers only a very limited form of peaceful protest. By 1882, as Zola was finishing *Germinal*, radicalism was dying in France; the 1881–82 French Socialist Party had split, and the left-to-center moderate majority rejected the extreme left-wing Marxists.

"GERMINAL" AS "THE CRUELLEST MONTH"

Germinal was originally published in 1885. The book's title is drawn from the calendar of the French Revolution of 1789, "Germinal" being the revolutionary month of April. This ever-recurring month of April is one of Zola's most fully sustained mythic symbols, this "cruellest month" anticipating T. S. Eliot's *The Waste Land* being Emile Zola's primary fertility-death symbol.

An easily accessible paperback edition of *Germinal* is available from Garnier-Flammarion publishers of Paris, and it is being increasingly used in college French courses. The considerably more expensive, annotated critical edition of the *Bibliotheque de la Pleiade of Gallimard* of the entire Rougon-Macquart is available in most university libraries. The novel is available in a modern English version translated by Stanley and Eleanor Hochman, and it is available in a New American Library "Signet Classic" paperback edition. Also, the famous Tancock translation is published in paperback by Penguin.

English translations contained in this Note are originals by this commentator.

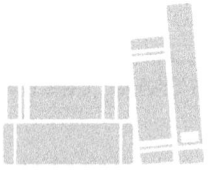

GERMINAL

. . . .

ZOLA'S USE OF THE "PROLOGOS"

Parts I and II of *Germinal* contain eleven chapters, six and five respectively, which concern themselves with an outsider-narrator, similar to Zola himself as he visited such strike-ridden towns of Northern France as Anzin, in search of notes for his novel. We become gradually acquainted with the narrator's new way of life as we follow Etienne Lantier through Zola's first ten chapters, from his arrival at Montsou to the conclusion of his first day of work in the mines. In this intimate time closeup, we absorb considerable **exposition** and technical detail with regard to the story's background, setting, and immediate circumstances in Zola's presentation of a kind of tragic "prologos" which eventually filters into nearly one fourth of the novel's content. The eleventh chapter, the fifth and last of Part II, draws us back from the preliminary ten-chapter closeup through Lantier's consciousness, to a vaguely omniscient wide angle montage of

Montsou as the novel's narrative consciousness backs off for the broadly distant view.

ZOLA'S NARRATIVE TECHNIQUE

Basically, *Germinal* is an "omniscient" narrative of traditional third-person form, presented through the character-consciousness of Etienne Lantier. His arrival at the desolate mining town gradually brings to a head the conflict between capital and labor which ultimately brings an untimely end to many of his friends. Lantier is, at first, immediately accepted as a friend and lodger of the Maheu family; and, he is eventually applauded by the miners as a leader. He first hears the mysterious story of the mines from Old Bonnemort and then has the direct experience of the mines. His first day below, however, finds Etienne in a hostile relationship with Chaval, who becomes his rival in a triangle involving Catherine, the Maheus' daughter. Likewise, when the strike is called, it is Lantier who arouses the particular animosity of the "rentiers," the mine-company stockholders. Considerable information might be given at this point concerning Etienne Lantier's hereditary background, but close study of *Germinal* in the context of the other Rougon-Macquart novels will reveal that it is the most self-contained and independent novel of Zola's cycle. *Germinal* is one of the exceptional "romans clos" of the cycle, containing a comparative lack of emphasis on hereditary afflictions. This is one of the positive characteristics of the major working class novels of Zola's colossal "roman fleuve"; these include *Germinal*, *La Terre* (The Earth), *La Bete Humaine* (The Human Beast), and *La Debacle* (The Debacle). There is, however, a slight seepage of the hereditary strain into *Germinal* in Lantier's inherited temper which has precipitated his being fired from the railroad.

ZOLA'S MODES OF ARTISTIC SELECTION

The early chapters of *Germinal* are of great significance because they promptly reveal to us Zola's modes of artistic selection. Zola's fiction is exemplary of the tradition of "scientisme," but a purely scientific portrayal of life would be virtually impossible, for a true-to-life portrayal of the world in the manner of "scientisme" would involve itself with an unwieldy attempt at life-totality, involving all socioeconomic strata, including all human types, with a broad expanse of chronological history. Certain modes of artistic selection, however, become immediately evident in *Germinal*. They are introduced in the early chapters and are sustained throughout the work. These modes of selection include those indebted to Zola's Mediterranean roots in Classicism which included his Aix-en-Provence education which gave him a full understanding of Greek myths, Homeric epics, and Athenian tragedies. Zola's modes of artistic selection also include those indebted to Zola's ties with the Romantic tradition, with its accent on imagination and lyricism, and the works of its great French master, Victor Hugo. Many critics feel that the Emile Zola who wrote in the shadow of the Romantic imagination, with its creative figurative language, was Emile Zola the master. In his famous letter to Henry Ceard, one of the younger writers of his celebrated Medan Circle, Zola himself admitted that, despite the effort at scientific representation and analysis, there was still an element of the "lie" in creative writing: this was, in fact, inherent in Zola's vision of creation, his conception of **metaphor**. Finally, of Emile Zola's most significant modes of artistic selection, is that rooted in the objectively neutral, "innocent eye" scientific method of the Impressionists. In the visual arts, Impressionism was basically conceived of as an extension of **Realism** and as a basic counter-movement against the lyrical subjectivity and sentimentalism of the Romantics.

GENERAL INTRODUCTION OF ZOLA'S USE OF IMPRESSIONISM

As a basically objectified, de-sentimentalized approach to color manipulation and everyday subject matter, Impressionistic technique is preeminent in Zola's presentation of the treeless Montsou landscape swept by March winds, and in his placing of the begrimed miners in thick impasto against the grey sfumato backdrop. In the manner of the Impressionists, Zola has presented huge brush-strokes of the primary colors of red, blue, and green (or yellow) against backdrops of either black or white, leaving their spectral effects in basically scientific technique before the reader. The Impressionists often used adjacent primaries to create intermediate spectral color sensations, as Zola has at times done with yellow or purple in the midst of adjacent reds and greens or reds and blues. Varying quantities of the primaries may also interact additively or subtractively to create sensations of white light or spectral black. Like the viewer of the Impressionistic canvas, the reader of Zola is presented with material innovatively arranged in a break from romanticism and sentimental realism, material scientifically and impartially set forth before his neutral "innocent eye" from which he himself is to derive his own conclusions. Zola also used the technique of a Renaissance inventor and scientifically-minded artistic genius, Leonardo da Vinci, in his vague representation of a line which the viewer concludes to be a horizon line in the technique of chiaroscuro. The landscape appears in a chiaroscuro effect amid misty greys and shadowy blacks, Etienne Lantier not quite being able to see the vast horizon. The reader can only scarcely see the road amid the spectral shadows, and Le Voreux only vaguely begins to emerge from the night as we approach it. Uniquely Impressionistic, also, was Emile Zola's fascination by the effects and natural laws of weather conditions in his coloration of landscapes.

ZOLA'S USE OF IMPRESSIONISTIC COLOR CONTRASTS

Much of Part I of *Germinal* is suffused in the Impressionistic use of contrast, bringing forth bright primary colors subtractively absorbed into a somberly neutral or blackish background. We frequently see, for instance, red flame set against a dark backdrop in the portrayals of the figuratively volcanic Le Voreux as the fiery Biblical Moloch of the Montsou nights. As well as frequently juxtaposing red and black, with their obvious associations with hellfire and doom, Zola likewise utilized a very technically strategic introduction of spectral yellow in the apocalyptic figure of the yellow horse. White and yellow, as well as other light pastel-like colors, emerge as the archetypal colors of apocalypse in *Germinal* and serve to generate apocalypse as a general **theme** of the book as a whole. Set against the recurring yellow motif are the intensely compelling reds and blues of the everburning blast furnaces and coke ovens.

ZOLA'S DEBT TO CLASSICAL DRAMA

Among the modes of artistic selection revealed in the early chapters of *Germinal* are those indicative of Zola's Classical dramatic consciousness. Zola had been an excellent student of the Classics and had written plays upon numerous occasions. The first ten chapters of *Germinal* serve to present **exposition** in much the same manner as a choric "prologos," which precedes the first **episode** or act, in which the plot itself advances. While Zola actually considered the Homeric **epic** to be the direct ancestor of the modern novel, he did adhere to the spirit of the Classical tragedians as much as was possible for a novelist. His brand of time unity does not keep us within the Aristotelian ideal of twenty-four hours, but it does bear the cyclical mythopoetic spirit of that unity in his handling of the time-span of roughly a year in his story. Rather than going from sun to sun, as in a day, we go from bitter spring through bitter harvest to bitter spring. Unity of place is self-evident as is the unity and simplicity of the solidly packed plot, a basic five-act type plot with numerous elements of Euripidean "deus ex machina" in the patent determinism of events. Like Homer and the Athenian tragedians, Zola often alluded to ancient myths and archetypes in such material as the regeneration **theme**, the general references to the Underworld, and the specific **allusions** to Ceres, Cyclops, and Tartarus.

ZOLA'S ARTISTIC ESTABLISHMENT OF ATMOSPHERE

Much controversy has arisen regarding the overall artistic quality of Zola's Rougon-Macquart, many critics considering even *Germinal* to be wearisome and predictable. However, there is a profusion of artistic passages of first-class creative authenticity in the cycle, as Zola stepped forth from his professed scientific detachment and assumed the full responsibilities of the artist, taking care not to lapse into moralistic or propagandistic incursions. Examples of such first-class metaphorical passages appear early in *Germinal* as the archetypal rhythms of annihilation manifest themselves in such imagery as the scythe, a death symbol associated with the harsh March wind; the black sea, a **metaphor** associated with the desolate plain; and the various personifications associated with breathing, panting, and coughing. In giving creative strength to his ever-present environment, Zola gave environmental factors an overwhelmingly claustrophobic and imprisoning atmosphere, giving the reader to feel that the characters are inextricably trapped. The leaden sky gives even the smoldering flames the apparition-like appearance of vaguely smoky, cloudy moons. Along with the supernatural play of light, we find a sensitively wrought description of the incipiently senile Bonnemort in which Zola suggested that his premature age itself might well have precipitated his sad conversation-lapse with Lantier, pathetic ramblings rooted in some strangely unexplainable impulse to talk. Like the yellow horse, Old Bonnemort is a determined victim of the mines who went down as a young man and who, after forty-five years underground, came up as a partially paralyzed old man.

ZOLA'S ANTICIPATION OF EXISTENTIALISM

Early in *Germinal*, Zola made use of the words "le vide" ("emptiness" / "nothingness") and "neant" ("nothingness") which anticipated later authors, particularly the Existentialists among whom mention could be made of the pre-Existentialist Marcel Proust, and the masters of the school, Andre Gide and Jean-Paul Sartre. Interestingly, Andre Gide considered *Germinal* one of the ten best novels ever written; it is a novel far ahead of its time in such respects as its thematic concern with the existential and the apocalyptic. As we enter Zola's subterranean depths, we discover that the void, the nothingness, is the elemental reality of the mines. The characters must deal singly with their anxiety and desperation in the isolated mining town. As the town itself is cut off from the mainstream of life, the miners are likewise cut off from life and daylight. The sense of solitude is of **epic** scale, and it is significant that the Montsou dwellers are ever conscious of themselves as a community. What consolation does come to them comes to them in their sense of community, in their numbers. *Germinal*, as a whole, could be interpreted from a modern standpoint as a novel of "consciousness"; it is the story of the miners' becoming collectively aware of themselves and of their potential amid the adversity of the surroundings. After the suffering and despair which come with the strike repression comes a kind of consciousness and inner identity. The men who are to collectively attain this consciousness become truly alive; they are to conquer nothingness and attain dignity. Jean-Paul Sartre spoke of "nothingness" in his *L'Etre et le Neant* (Being and Nothingness) of 1943, and one may cite several references to "neant" and its synonyms in *Germinal*. One of the earliest in the book appears in the description of "le vide," the "void" or "emptiness" of a despairing cartman's blank extinguished eyes (Part I, ch. 1). In the truly modern and existential sense, *Germinal* is a quest novel dealing with the meaning of life. The incipient affirmation at the end reveals to us as to what it is that drives men to go on in the face of atrocious living and working conditions amid the ever-present inevitability of death.

ESTABLISHMENT OF ENVIRONMENTAL DETAILS

Mention has already been made of Zola's debt to ancient Athens in his conception of *Germinal's* "prologos," but mention should also be made of the profusion of specific details emanating from the prologue and its major narrative vehicles. Of particular significance is the profusion of expository detail presented to us by the archetypal miner, the choric elder of Montsou, Old Bonnemort. Zola serves to effectively establish the novel's **epic** and tragic characteristics through Bonnemort by setting his mysterious story against the great environmental monoliths of the immense horizon, the existential solitude of Montsou, and the ravenousness of La Voreux. As well as the descriptions of the mine complex, the "prologos" presents to us the basic plot nucleus of the whole book: the fact that the period in history is one of severe economic depression and extremely high unemployment. There were no welfare benefits for the unemployed, no fringe benefits for the employed, and no collective bargaining units to inhibit wage and labor abuses. The mining town is much like a ghetto; its dwellers are cut off from the mainstream of any fluid economy because virtually every small business enterprise is absentee-owned by the vaguely nebulous and malevolent company whose directors operate in Paris. One of the cruelest manifestations of this distant company ownership becomes evident in the figure of Maigrat, the company storekeeper who is the greedy archenemy of the community.

ZOLA'S POLITICAL NEUTRALITY

It was with publication of *Germinal*, which inaugurated a succession of powerful working-class novels, that Emile Zola came to be labeled a socialist writer. He, however, dealt with the blame factor in the workers' plight in a technically interesting way. Inherent in the author's objective and supposedly neutral method is an attempt to equitably distribute the causal factors over a wide range of uncontrollable deterministic elements. More significantly, however, we discover that, impartial as Zola attempted to be, nearly all of the blame factors fall on the inherent properties of the capitalist system. In the light of present-day Marxism, however, Zola's leanings to the left seem quite bland, and contemporary critics like the Hungarian Marxist, George Lukacs, consider the evident lack of commitment as a major flaw in Zola's work. The finger of blame points at the "laissez faire" capitalist system in general: even M. Hennebeau, the "rentier" general-manager at Montsou, is in his own way as much a victim of the industrial complex as other hirelings. Thus, by distributing blame relatively evenly, Zola avoids the overly simplistic and propagandistic approach of much of the later Marx-inspired literature, especially that extending between the World Wars to the mid-twentieth century. When Etienne asks Old Bonnemort who owns the mine complex, his answer is merely a quizzical reference to "gens," to some vague and unidentified group of "people" (Part I, Ch. 1). These are the emissaries of the system with all of its natural laws of boom and recession, profit and loss, polarization of bourgeoisie and proletariat-natural laws which have attained to godhead and have usurped the tabernacle. Capitalism has abandoned the theological God for the economic god-substitute which seems to promise so much to the bourgeoisie, but which is so far from being infallible. Zola presented capitalism as being not only fallible, but also self-destroying in the Marxist sense as are his huge architectural and mechanical monoliths-his mammoths of engineering draftsmanship and technical design. The mine itself is symbolized as some **epic** beast, a kind of Homeric Cyclops-like carnivore which, like the capitalist system, will ultimately fall in upon itself.

ZOLA'S MONTSOU AS ARTISTIC CREATION

The reader of *Germinal* is drawn from a panoramic view of Montsou Village Number 240 as set against a black nighttime sky at four A. M. on a cold Monday morning, into a closeup of the homely details of the Maheu household. The prominent and sustained motif of crushing weight proliferates in the description of the poverty-stricken home, Number 16 of Block 2. Environment is so overwhelmingly prison-like to these humble people that even the addresses themselves seem like cellblock numbers. While chapter two takes us through the overcrowded home of the Maheus with its cold, hungry children and its young female forced to work underground, chapter three takes us to the mine itself at four A. M. work-time, bringing Etienne and the Maheus together, after which the foreman is persuaded to take him on as temporary help.

From an artistic standpoint, there is material in chapter two which is frequently overlooked but which is nevertheless masterful. In terms of artistic selection, Zola used his color device effectively to suggest the cold and overpowering bleakness of the laborers' lot. As chapter one brought us the yellow horse, this chapter brings us a pervasive presence of the off-white of anemic pallor and blonde hair. Likewise, in subsequent chapters, Zola was to frequently use white light against additive primary colors as a phantom color, a color with negative X-ray effect juxtaposed and often symbolically equated with black. The mine shafts are black as are the coal and the ever-present coal dust which not only contaminates the lungs of the workers but which ceaselessly poses the threat of instantaneous combustion triggered by methane firedamp, released by the disturbance and displacement of coal lodes.

Despite the fact that there are certain passages in Zola bearing such artistic flaws as excessive repetition and overextended description, there are those which are so exceptional in their artistic authenticity and imaginative subtlety that they anticipate the full fruition of post-Symbolist and post-Expressionist Naturalism which was to emerge in the United States with such writers as John Steinbeck. Memorable is the lean exactitude of the powerfully suggestive and economical description of Catherine as she leaves home for her brutalizing job in the mine: "elle avait l'air d'un petit homme" / "she seemed like some little man" (Part I, Ch. 2). We also feel the overwhelming impact of La Maheude's sad remark to Catherine as the latter illuminates the room full of Monday morning darkness: "je n'ai pas besoin de voir la couleur de mes idees" / "I don't have to see the color of my thoughts" (Part I, Ch. 2). In numerous strategic places, Zola likewise made masterful use of the suggestive quality of things "falling back," as in the case of the room furnishings which "etaient retombes aux tenebres" / "would fall back into the darkness" (Part I, Ch. 2) with the extinguishing of the candle.

ZOLA'S TECHNOLOGICAL AND ARTISTIC MASTERY

Part I brings us to the actuality of the mine itself with Zola presenting to us some superlative technical description of the mine operations. The author's scientific-mindedness lent itself well to the objective specifications of the mine-shaft machinery. The lift-engine is a four-hundred-horsepower monster reeling and unreeling singing cables on wheels five times the height of a man. Amid the brute force of machinery which lifts and drops men, horses, and materials some five hundred and fifty-four meters (eighteen hundred and twenty-eight feet), Zola's writing has unexpected grace when we read of the weight and velocity specifications of the cable: it lifts some eleven thousand kilograms (fifty-thousand pounds) at the rate of ten meters (thirty feet) per second, and later in the novel Zola used superlative bird **imagery** in metaphorical descriptions of the cable. The overwhelming noise of the resounding mine activity is presented with incisiveness and precision as we hear the general tumult of hammer blows, bells ringing, and machines whirring, and it is further enhanced by the ominous silence with which the elevator cage descends, "tombait comme un pierre, ne laissait derriere elle que la fuite vibrant du cable" / "would fall like a stone, and would leave behind it just the vibrant running away of the cable" (Part I, Ch. 3). We are led into a brief passage of frightening fatalism, fraught with a hopeless determinism as the miners chance to contemplate possible mine accidents as Etienne inquires as to what might happen were the cable ever to break. Zola's Naturalist technique functions nearly perfectly here as the author leaves the deterministic answer up to the reader: "Ah! quand ca casse ..." / "Ah! When it breaks..." (Part I, Ch. 3).

Zola masterfully continued the "falling away" motif, allowing it to follow into Etienne's first ride in the lift which suddenly gives a jolt upon first starting, giving surrounding objects the illusion of "s'envolerent" / "would fly away" as birds taking wing. Lantier rapidly drops past a cave layer, and experiences the existential sensation of "nothingness" as "on retombait au neant" / "one would fall back into nothingness" (Part I, Ch. 3). There is also something resembling the existential imperative in Zola's detached prose, making it incumbent upon the reader to determine choices and priorities amid the existentialist trademark of "mean." The author used his color selection metaphorically in describing Richomme, using the color yellow to highlight the old foreman's eyes, which we see first before any other details of the man are presented. As well as the suggestions of "nothingness," and the "falling away" motif, Zola also effectively used storm **imagery** in his description of the internal mine activity. Zola's debt to the Impressionists is manifest not only in his use of primary color, but also in his predilection for weather conditions in his landscape and metaphorical images. Chapter four continues out of chapter three as we experience a compelling day in the mine as seen through the "innocent eye" of the newcomer. From a creative standpoint, Zola selected the figure of Catherine as one basic contrastive element of description, highlighting her against the grim backdrop of the mine by the grotesque effect of strategic color contrasts. In describing the mine, Zola selected red and black and enhanced the effect by setting off the "noir inconnu" / "unknown black" against the "formes spectrales" / "phantom forms" (Part I, Ch. 4) in a subtle placement of black against white, which extends into a reference to the "reflet de crystal" / "crystal reflection" of the coal itself. As the prose gathers relentless momentum, Catherine herself is blended into the color contrasts as black coal dust covers her body from which her teeth exude a strange whiteness. Complementary colors are also used Impressionistically in Catherine's depiction as we see reddish hair against greenish eyes. The background proliferates in strong hues of red and a vivid, gassy blue as the mine lamps keep the heavy drafts of firedamp fumes in check. Zola also made interesting, almost synesthetic use of light and sound effects reverberating about in the claustrophobic mine.

LABOR-MANAGEMENT RELATIONS

Chapters five and six present to us the details of the payment adjustments which have been effected by the company to implement periodic maintenance of the timbered mine casings. The workers are angered at what is the company's obvious disguised pay cut, for which the recession itself is actually most responsible. Specifically, the workers' timbering job, the "boisage," is to be paid for separately, and the redemption price for each cartload, each "berline," is to be cut by ten centimes. This is the company's shrewd way of cutting its own costs by forcing a greater burden on the workers by paying separately for the timbering, payments which could not offset the price cut of the cartloads. Consequently, the miners must hurry as fast as they can at both jobs, doing sloppy repairs on the timbering and taking extra risks in the mine to make up for the lost pay. One of the stark facts which make *Germinal* so sadly deterministic is the inevitable futility of a strike during an economic recession when those fortunate enough to be employed are the most at the mercy of those who have hired them. As we become more and more exposed to the misery purveyed on workers by labor exploitation, Emile Zola's uniquely rampant literary style shifts into high gear as we already see the indignation and seed of rebellion in the only partially educated but highly articulate Etienne Lantier.

MODERNISM IN ZOLA'S APOCALYPTIC HORSE

One of the singular masterpieces of Zola's vivid prose is his unabating description of the pathetic Bataille, Impressionistically depicted by light-dark contrasts that are, in fact, so penetrating that there is a prefiguring of Expressionism suffusing the entire sequence. As unoriginal as reference to Pablo Picasso's "Guernica" may be, the apocalyptic signaling of a kind of Surrealistic nightmare of **dehumanization** and annihilation is spellbinding in its anticipation of twentieth-century post-Naturalist authors. A vastly Kafkan atmosphere of the subconscious pervades in the passage relating the descent of Bataille, and it exudes the atmosphere of Proustian involuntary memory as well. The unfortunate horse experiences a delirium of heightened consciousness upon seeming to recall the nearly forgotten sun, "l'odeur oubliee du soleil" / "the forgotten fragrance of the sun" with the "joie de ces choses anciennes" / "joy of days long gone by" (Part I, Ch. 5). There is a terrifying similarity between this moment and the last moment of little Alzire's life about which we read later in the novel as the tiny hunchback dies horribly in delirium tremens from cold and starvation. There is little wonder as to why men in history have risen in revolt.

ARTISTIC CONCLUSION OF PART ONE

We are introduced to numerous characters during Etienne's first day at Montsou, one of whom is a certain innkeeper named Rasseneur who figures significantly in the story by his position concerning the rising tide of protests. His hostelry is set against the background of coal-black and fire-red amid varying degrees of iron-greys by Zola's again using the primary colors in the inn's objective presentation: red brick, blue window frames, and the yellow sign-lettering reading "L'Avantage." We become introduced by side references to a radical named Pluchart, and momentum increases by further reference to the economic depression, a seemingly self-evident inevitability of the ultimately self-destructing machinery of capitalism. Technically, Zola would theoretically appear to be impartial and objective in his narrative, but his Marx-influenced sympathy to the left is all but transparent. The reader who understands the biography of Zola, however, can well understand the author's distrust of the capitalist bourgeoisie as well as his fear of and compassion for the proletariat.

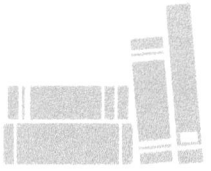

GERMINAL

....

PART TWO

ZOLA'S CONTRASTIVE SYMMETRY

The beginning of Part II marks an artistic shift of focus from Part I, and it illustrates Zola's debt to Classicism in his development of symmetry in his modes of artistic selection. The author's balancing of the glimpse into the Maheu home at rising-time against his contrastive glimpse into the Gregoire home at their later and more leisurely rising-time bears a Classical symmetry of unparalleled leanness and literary economy. Despite the fact that, at times, Zola's works lapse into prosaic excesses, they are at other times as compressed and clear as those of the exemplary Realist, Gustave Flaubert. As Part I began and ended symmetrically with panoramas of the landscape, we see in Part II a symmetrical view of the household routine at the well-to-do Gregoires' house as set in a terrifying contrast against the routine of the poverty-stricken Maheus back on the same Monday morning. Little does one know yet of the intersecting paths which will yet bring Cecile

Gregoire and Old Bonnemort together in one highly strategic later **episode**. It is also significant that we see not only the home scene, but also the mining scene through the naive eyes of the rich Gregoires, conservative stockholders of the Montsou Company-people who, unlike the also well-to-do Hennebeaus, have never worked or even seen real work in their lives. The superlative concentration of Zola's prose in the Gregoire rising and breakfasting sequence is reminiscent of Flaubert, with its purity of form honed almost to the point of "le mot juste" as exemplified in the concentrated strategic focus upon the exquisite pastry, the brioche. This culinary focal point in the kitchen marks a tragically vivid contrast between the Maheu and the Gregoire lifestyles-heightened by the pathetically ineffectual charity-donation of part of the brioche to La Maheude who has arrived at great expense to her pride for a small monetary advance to carry her through the week. She has literally dragged two of her hungry children through cold mud to the plush 700-acre estate of the Gregoires, "La Paoline."

FINANCIAL BACKGROUND OF GREGOIRE FAMILY

With Zola's mastery of objective prose and keen observation for technical detail, a sizeable section of Part II's first chapter is devoted to the historical and financial background of the Gregoire's inheritance which dates back to an investment of savings amounting to 10,000 francs in the purchase of a share of the original Montsou mine stock on the part of Leon Gregoire's great grandfather. With the consolidation and huge financial success of the Montsou shares, the value of the original Gregoire investment compounds in value by fivefold inside of one hundred years of the Montsou Company's formation, seeing three generations of the family through extraordinary wealth and promising it for succeeding generations as well.

IMPRESSIONISTIC USE OF WHITE

As Zola points up the economic contrast of the Maheus and the Gregoires with consummate skill, he likewise makes consummate use of his primary colors in his Gregoire chapters. Set against an elegant white, as contrasted with the dusty black of the workers, the affluent grand bourgeoisie languishes in crisp, fresh whiteness. They regard their financial wealth as almost divinely infallible, as almost inherent in natural law that they be bestowed with wealth; and as we look on at the pampered Cecile, there is some vaguely distant forecast of doom in the elaborations upon her comfort and security. With Cecile, Part II brings to the reader a range of colors beyond the heretofore predominant red and black. Amid the grey Zolaesque backdrop, we find increased references to blue, not the blue of gas lamps but a delicate blue crossed into the upper-class white motif, a pastel shade of whitish blue. It is, gradually and ominously, to become the lovely and innocent Cecile's color-ironically soft, rustling, angelic. However, as we see La Maheude dragging her two small children along the road, we see an interesting interaction of the miner's red and black again as we return to the sustained backdrop of the cold plain, this time in full somber daylight. The fields are reddish, the houses are brick, and they are trimmed in yellow or blue, ultimately to turn black. Zola's use of the bold impasto strokes and heavy daubs of primary colors here is consummate: our minds gather up the color patches and assemble the ultimate effect in Impressionistic color constructs.

MONTSOU POPULACE AS SEEN BY MAHEUS

It is in Part II's second chapter that we follow along with the Maheus, observing their encounter with Cecile Gregoire and her pathetic effort at charity, meeting the terrible Maigrat, and meeting the ineffectual Abbe Joire. His begrimed church seems to bespeak a death of Christianity in this hopelessly impoverished community. Cecile's obliviousness in chapter two is to be set off in an interesting symmetrical balance, of which the reader becomes aware only upon reading the entire novel, with another charity incident involving her well-intentioned but culpably oblivious donation of shoes to the crippled Bonnemort. And as we cross paths with the exploitative colluder with the company establishment, the storekeeper Maigrat, and the cowardly Abbe Joire, we see a ferocious colorless sky swirling above the fiercely courageous and proudly dignified La Maheude. The restraint which we see in La Maheude at this point in the novel is eventually to give way to a similarly ferocious swirling bitterness as exemplified in threatening sky and cold mud.

As Part II progresses, one can see among other details of the Montsou populace, the total blankness of church worship. The laws of capitalism seem to have taken the power out of the traditional theological God's hands: the tabernacle has been usurped. The mechanical quality of the service is marked by the fact the Abbe Joire comes to "dire" / "say" Mass on Sundays rather than to celebrate it. We observe, likewise, Zola's introduction of a **theme** that has heretofore been mentioned only briefly and obliquely. A **theme** eventually to reach volcanic proportions is that of Maigrat's demands on those to whom he has grudgingly extended credit. Catherine Maheu is made the focal point of this **theme** through subtle, suspicious remarks suggesting that hers is a role of being some sort of collateral in La Maheude's credit. The mother does not wish to declare this fact to her daughter by bluntly telling her, so she cautions Catherine to avoid the Maigrat store under the pretense that his ribbons are inferior.

ARTISTIC TREATMENT OF STRIKE PREPARATIONS

Chapter five of Part II brings us to a culmination of the sufferings endured by the miners, preparatory to the miners' decision to strike which solidifies in Part III. Instrumental to this preparatory material is the description of the stockholding "rentier," Deneulin, and his mine, Jean Bart, by contrast with the Gregoires and Le Voreux. The basic tone of the chapter is darkly ominous, portending the eruption of revolution and violence which is accelerated at an ever-increasing momentum throughout the remainder of the novel. This fifth chapter serves to prepare us for the major turning-point of the novel, a kind of Classical crisis-climax which is to later come with its "peripeteia," as the workers gather the ferocity and resolve to actually dare to call a strike, drastic and practically unheard-of action at that time, particularly during a recession. Artistic devices contributing to the sustained rhythms of the leaden atmosphere include the motifs of darkness and night, accentuated by their falling as some cloud of smoke, contributing to the sfumato effect of grim landscape and gloomy climate. The primary colors again come into play as they do consistently through the book. The furious beet-red Maigrat shows Chaval and Catherine some blue ribbons, allowing our minds to Impressionistically deduce a livid purple in spectral effect. Later, Catherine appears in a dark blue dress which heightens Chaval's burning rage as he recognizes her greenish eyes. The final seething description of La Voreux of Part II is consummate as Zola made his most effective use of the play of eerie light on Bonnemort, the yellow horse, and the mine fires amid the backdrop of the somber plain and the ever-increasing darkness. Reminiscent of an earlier reference to the moon in smoke, we now see the braziers likened to moons in blood, sustaining Zola's powerful moon motif amid the again-burning flames of blue and red of the blast-furnaces and coke-ovens. Finally, there is an onslaught of darkness on the plain, likened to existential "neant" / "nothingness" (Part II, Ch. 5).

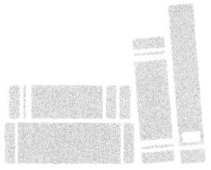

GERMINAL

. . . .

ZOLA'S MARX-INFLUENCED CHARACTERS

Most significant to the student's understanding of Part III is the previous brief explanation of the pay scale introduced to the miners which is but the triggering incident which sets the already tense situation into irrevocable motion. In Part III, both time and events pass rapidly. We pass from the March signaled at the beginning of the book, into the months which give full blossom to Zola's cruel spring, into the summer months as life takes a kind of deterministic natural course with the growing intensification of revolutionary fervor. Part III brings references to the International Workingmen's Association into play as well as bringing the Bakunin-disciple, Souvarine, into prominent play. One familiar with the various Socialist movements in France up to the World War I period may take ready notice of the influence of Russia through Marxism in such Socialist groups as Jules Guesde's "Guesdists," forms of left-wing anarchism, the "Possibilists," and the later "Syndicalists."

As well as bringing us face to face with Souvarine and the London International, Part III brings to us the sustained **theme** of germination as well as a masterfully artistic recurrence of bird-imagery associated with the cable motif, "les cables qui filaient d'une aile noir et muette d'oiseau nocturne" / "the cables which would run away like some night bird's mute black wings" (Part III, Ch. 1). A previous outstanding reference to the bird motif appears in Part I, Chapter 4, as we hear in the mine "un leger bouillonnement ... pareil a un sifflement d'oiseau" / "a soft fluttering ... like a flurry of birds." It is in Part III, however, that *Germinal* begins to emerge as a novel of "consciousness" as it takes on a vastly international flavor in establishing the fact that the proletariat's struggle is world-wide and not just confined to Montsou. We are prepare for the revolt as a mass movement with its mob scenes which are among Zola's masterpieces.

SOUVARINE AS EXISTENTIAL ANARCHIST

Souvarine is presented ironically in terms of the same pastel shades that hover over the Gregoires, except that Souvarine's are more strident, suggestive of the ultimate tragic intersection of the paths of the bourgeoisie and the proletariat. Souvarine is also presented as a fully developed existential character anticipating twentieth-century characters such as the tragically deterministic anti-heroes of such works as *La Condition Humaine* (Man's Fate) by Andre Malraux. Psychologically scarred by the brutal oppression of czarist Russia, Souvarine has developed from existential fear to existential indifference, a nihilistic detachment as manifest in his lifestyle as a transient. Souvarine is also fraught with the torments of solitude, an overwhelmingly deterministic isolation which he hopes to shatter by giving himself to the anarchist cause, a kind of dignity-seeking god-substitute which he himself does not really understand. Later in the novel, Souvarine is to act with the same blind sense of fatalism as Ch'en in *Man's Fate* as he detonates a bomb in front of a decoy car amid the desolate civil war-ridden metropolis Shanghai. Souvarine's "modus operandi" is the left-wing extremist's credo that the end justifies the means, an extreme form of activism which makes Zola's prose shudder as much as the author himself probably did. As time passes in Part III, Etienne hears more and more Marxist propaganda. Being articulate but only semi-educated, he falls an easy prey to its high-flown promises of such nebulous abstractions as a new world rising from the rubble of the old destroyed world, etc. The author's assimilation of phraseology from the *Communist Manifesto* is more than obvious in the utterances of the apparently brainwashed Souvarine.

ALZIRE MOTIF AS A RECURRING DEVICE

The powerful suggestion of redolent memory plays upon little Alzire, much as it did upon the horse Bataille in the earlier sequence. Zola's reference to Alzire plays a significant role in forecasting the manner of her death. It is in the recurring and blended motifs that the author gives his novel much of its **epic** quality; the ancient epics contained frequent repetition on account of the fact that these long stories were imparted orally.

POLARIZATION OF PLUCHART AND RASSENEUR

As the seasons progress in *Germinal* into the grim winter preparations of October, the Pluchart-Rasseneur conflict crystalizes and gives way to a mass resolution in favor of activism. The rhetoric of work-stoppage escalates as Etienne takes his place among the activitists as Rasseneur's moderate position is overruled by the angry miners. It is at this point in *Germinal* that the crowd begins to solidify into a unit, becoming a sort of collective character. It had begun to solidify somewhat in July as it enjoyed a collective mood of raucous fun, a feeling of fun determined not to last long past the summer festival and determined to end emphatically with the approach of December 1, the day on which the new pay-arrangement is to take effect. It is surely due to the miner's deterministic awareness of things to come that they abandon themselves so completely when an opportunity for pleasure presents itself.

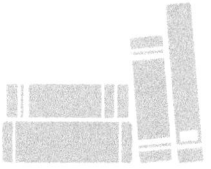

GERMINAL

. . . .

HENNEBEAU'S PERSONAL MISERY

As Part III propelled itself to the miners' resolve to strike, Part IV presents the dramatic **climax** of the strike itself. This detonating incident is set against the genteel tapestry of Mme. Hennebeau's luncheon party celebrating the engagement of M. Hennebeau's nephew to Cecile, the rich shareholder's daughter. One of Emile Zola's most sensitively wrought stories is woven into the violence-torn fabric of the strike, the story of M. Hennebeau"s unsuccessful marriage. Despite their wealth, we feel compassion for the Hennebeaus because they are at least self-made, not being wealthy through heredity as are the Gregoires, and M. Hennebeau captures reader-sympathy because we discover his misfortune through his consciousness simultaneously as he does. The shock comes not only with the sad discovery concerning his wife but with that concerning his nephew, Paul Negrel, as well.

Zola makes effective use of Impressionist colorations in reflecting not only the heightened emotional states of the characters, but in permeating such names as Le Rouge and Negrel with red and black. The latter's name is to symbolically strike the death-knell for the sanctity of the Hennebeau marriage, as M. Hennebeau is to stand alone amid the spectre of a rising crowd outside his window in Mme. Hennebeau's absence as sse goes to find the guest of honor, Cecile. The prose is strenuously neutral and Naturalistic, and yet it is artistically imaginative with its cold colorations associated with the Hennebeaus and the **allusion** to the grain goddess, Ceres, in the description of the still attractive Mme. Hennebeau as an autumnal Ceres. M. Hennebeau seems even to envy the raw coarseness of the promiscuous miners as he contemplates the lost illusions of his own life. Here, we see the lack of fulfillment in the lives of the rich as well as the poor of Montsou.

IRONY IN LIBERALISM AND CONSERVATISM

One of the heaviest ironies of *Germinal* comes when M. Gregoire professes to be a liberal at the Hennebeau's lavish party. The sad **irony** lies, of course, in the fact that none of the Gregoires have even the vaguest notion as to the scale of the worker's unrest and what this monumental sense of revolt could bring the workers to do. Upon entering the Hennebeaus' house, M. Gregoire shrugs his shoulders and dismisses the gathering mine workers as basically harmless, attributing to them his own well-mannered gentility by alluding to the decency of the miners, naively presuming that they would not even dream of any sort of striking or violence. Almost as sadly ironic as M. Gregoire's oblivious pseudo-liberalism is M. Deneulin's conservatism. While such stockholders in the big companies like Montsou's Gregoires reap the fruits of "laissez-faire" capitalism, aided and abetted by governmental conservatism, Deneulin is virtually ruined by big business. As a small businessman, he can ill afford to have his equipment damaged by the strikers, but the monster that will devour Jean Bart will be the capitalist establishment rather than the liberal wing.

THE HENNEBEAU-MAHEU CONFRONTATION

The brief second chapter of Part IV signals the coming of the major turning-point of *Germinal* as M. Hennebeau refuses the striker's peaceful requests by giving Maheu, their spokesman, and obvious run-around. Maheu becomes the main character of this chapter as he unexpectedly, as much to his own surprise as to anyone's else, is transformed from within as his grievances flow forth in an unabated rush from his lips, casting even the most disinterested listener into a rapturous spell. When he is through, however, his dismissal is nevertheless evident, giving us added sympathy for Maheu as a passive worker turned courageous leader. The impact of this chapter lies in the intersection of the workers' lives and the bourgeoisie's lives as the begrimed miners enter the plush home of the executive's family with its profusion of richly burnished yellow and golden hues.

ZOLA'S CLOSEUP OF SOUVARINE

The work-stop-page being in effect, Zola focuses in on Souvarine again after a wide panoramic view of Village 240 and the quiet mines. The anarchist's radical Communist views become more readily apparent with his overt advocacy of the International and his reverence to the Russian anarchist, Bakunin, whom he calls "Bakunin the Exterminator." Souvarine declares that there will be world-wide proletarian revolution with its beginnings in what one might call a Mother Russia (Bakunin looks to the East); he declares that evolutionism will fail and that Bakunin will spearhead the International's crushing of the entire old world taking us back to some nascent community "sans forme" / a "formless" community (Part IV, Ch. 4). Zola, in his objective approach, is not advocating an overthrow that will purportedly destroy everything including nations, government, property, and religion; he is simply presenting Souvarine as a representative of the troubled community's populace, just as he presents other representative types like Gregoire, Hennebeau, Rasseneur, and Maheu. It, in fact, was the ultraradicalism of certain of the early Marx-oriented Socialists that caused so many of these leftwing parties to split in the Western European countries and to ultimately lose their radical thrust by World War I. We see, likewise, in *Germinal* the initial applause given to Pluchart and his apprentice, Lantier, turn to bitter scorn and contempt by the end of the novel.

ENVIRONMENT AS CAUSAL FACTOR

As Part IV progresses, we are given a vivid recounting of the miseries of a terrible wageless January during which the workers must eke out the very minimum of subsistence. The ferocious cold and frequent casualties rival those encountered in the grueling march to Russia in Leo Tolstoi's *War and Peace*, a literary masterpiece from which material even today continues to be unabashedly lifted. As Zola focuses on the rudeness of the living conditions in Montsou, he takes us temporarily away from the village scene to the cave hideaway of the boy-criminal, Jeanlin Maheu, in one of his finest descriptive sections. The sequence carries a hauntingly eerie quality as Etienne Lantier is invited to join Jeanlin in his subterranean refuge. It bears the Zolaesque apocalyptic white and hearkens the reader back to other passages in which severance from the life-giving sun is the main **theme**. Etienne, verging on being a fugitive himself, feels something strangely in common with Jeanlin amid this vaguely apocalyptic atmosphere of petrified white light tinged with yellow. In these bizarre surroundings, Zola created a strangely negative white as a black-opposite, giving a terrifying Surreal and Expressionistic X-Ray effect in this cave that was once its natural color of black. It is now, however, embalmed and petrified in a dusty, powdery white, exuding a frightening ethery smell of an abandoned coal mine; even its timbering seems petrified, giving off "une paleur jaune de marbre, franges de guipures blanchatres, de vegetations flaconneuses qui semblaient les draper d'une passementerie de soie et de perles" / "a yellow pallor of marble, fringed with white lace, with flaky vegetation which would seem to form a draped embroidery of silk and pearls" (Part IV, Ch. 6). The masterpiece is culminated with powerful and hauntingly other-worldly description of a whole underground civilization of insects which, like Jeanlin, have turned a grotesque white in adapting themselves to perpetual darkness. Zola has created swarms of "papillons blancs, des mouches et des araignees de niege, un population decolore, a jamais ignorante du soleil" / "white moths and flies amid snowy spider webs, a civilization without color, forever unaware of the sun" (Part IV, Ch. 6). These spectral creatures, like Darwin's species and Zola's Rougon and Macquart families, have adapted themselves by Natural Selection to the adversities of a sunless environment. Whitened by darkness, they flourish and proliferate.

LANTIER'S EMERGENCE AS STRIKE LEADER

Chapter seven marks the conclusion of Part IV, bringing Etienne Lantier into a position of activist leadership with the mine strikers, rising above the innkeeper Rasseneur in the workmen's favor by declaring that a moderate position would not work. Etienne's triumph sequence in the forest presents outstanding description as Zola again so effectively and yet economically described the darkness in terms of the moon which "allait eteindre les etoiles" / "would rise to extinguish the stars" (Part IV, Ch. 7). Lantier is at the pinnacle of his power, rising in status from a mere outsider to the leader of the Montsou community. Starting out with just theoretical fragments and an uneducated but voracious appetite for reading, Lantier comes to gain the confidence of the Maheus and eventually the village-at-large, making the final decision to strike himself. By the end of the chapter, we stand squarely on the threshold of the strike events themselves, as Deneulin takes on Belgian miners as scabs, workers willing to come in from outside and break a strike for employment. Because the Belgian miners were subjected to the worst mining conditions in Europe, they were frequently willing to work outside of Belgium under conditions considered to be substandard in the rest of Europe. The appearance of the scabs precipitates the sabotage of the Jean Bart machinery by the Montsou strikers.

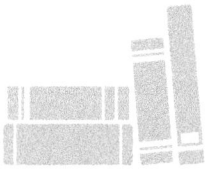

GERMINAL

. . . .

ZOLA'S DEBT TO CLASSICISM

It is in this section of *Germinal* that Emile Zola's **epic** magnitude becomes most evident in the scale of events, the relentlessness of the episodic material, and the profusion of **allusions** to ancient myths. In addition to the powerful Zolaesque color effects, there is also a substantial volume of material based on journalistic actuality, factual data gathered by the author in the mines of Northern France. The riot-torn town is suffused in red and black, and Zola gave Deneulin's Jean bart the kind of technical description that he gave to Le Voreux at the beginning of the book.

Zola's references to the Greek myths abound in *Germinal*, and the reference to Tartarus in "Tartaret" contributes to the **epic** quality of the novel. Anyone familiar with Tartarus is aware of its role as an underworld volcano similar to Hades, and anyone familiar with Zola is aware of the Gomorrah-like

"Tartaret's" role in Zola's credo of sexual morality. Even the most sensational of Zola's novels, such as *Nana*, bear out the credo that the abandonment of sexual morality will signal the end of civilization in general. One may, similarly, observe a heavy overlay of retribution in Zola's novels, and "Tartaret" exemplifies a kind of Dantesque-type of nether world with its Biblical fires engulfing the unspeakable transgressors. Marcel Proust was a direct heir of Zola in his descriptions of fires consuming those with hidden vices in his burning of Paris in the final volume of *Remembrance of Things Past*. In terms of color selection, "Tartaret" is described in heavy blotches of the typical Zolaesque yellow and red, set off by the green complementing red. To enhance his sense of the **epic**, the author adheres creditably to his scientifically detached method in his leaving with us Negrel's quizzical response to the strange atmosphere of the village. Zola leaves the inevitable guesswork as to the state of affairs up to the reader.

LANTIER'S TRAGIC "PERIPETEIA"

The tragic turning-point for Etienne Lantier and the Montsou miners is ironically preceded by his naive remark to La Maheude that his group's revolutionary action is not to endanger anyone's life. The crowd that has the young leader's total confidence is, as an unleashed group of protesters, unexpectedly to turn into an ugly uncontrollable mob. Zola was a master at imparting the idea that men in a mob situation have a completely different psychological make-up than men as private individuals. Etienne's following runs rampant, sabotages mine equipment, and becomes so threatening that the police are forced to overreact as Zola presents the tragic formula of numerous historic and recent civil disorders. After the mob has sliced Deneulin's mine-shaft cable, Deneulin interestingly attributes his ruin not to the strikers themselves, but to "une faute generale, seculaire" / "a general, secular fault," vague systematic failures in certain natural laws (Part V, Ch. 3).

SYMMETRY IN VIOLENT EPISODES

Set symmetrically against a D. H. Lawrence-type domestic sequence, involving Mme.

Hennebeau's infidelity to her sadly tormented and disillusioned husband, is the rise of the mob and the frighteningly symbolic emasculation of Maigrat. Chapter six of Part V is one of Emile Zola's most violent chapters in any of his works, ending with the appearance of the armed guardsmen. It, however, primarily involves itself with two symmetrically arranged strategic sequences, the first of which would seem almost amusing, but the second of which is unqualifiedly offensive. The chapter opens with a mild incident in which the pampered Cecile Gregoire is jostled but unharmed by the Montsou women as she proceeds to the Hennebeaus' party. As the chapter progresses, however, its content becomes increasingly violent. Despite this commentator's consternation with Zola's excesses in the Maigrat sequence, the scrupulous scholar might attribute some of the author's proclivities to his ties with the Greek myths and might even recognize a reworking of the ancient Kronos-Uranus story in the Maigrat **episode**. The band of retribution-bent Montsou wives' advance upon the company storekeeper resembles the advance upon the sleeping Uranus by Kronos. In the gory ancient myth, a group of hellish women spring forth from Uranus' defiled body-women strikingly similar to La Brule. The Zola retribution **theme** is obviously present with eye-for-an-eye simplicity. This second symmetrically arranged incident's peculiar and horrifying impact lies largely in the fact that the incident preceding it, in which Cecile only loses her veil and an amusingly small modicum of her modesty, is so startlingly and incongruously mild compared to the subsequent incident. The juxtaposition of the Maigrat incident against Hennebeau's impotence suggests outstanding artistic skill, as does the author's treatment of the entire Hennebeau sequence. The portrait of M. Hennebeau is unusually sensitive and is deserving of particularly high praise because Emile Zola was more the master of the collective character group than of the individual character. Rather than being a psychological author, he was a journalistic social commentator. Despite our horror at the violence of certain of Zola's episodes, nearly all of them were factually based on news actualities; and we must give the potent and torrential writer credit for breaking the silence of centuries.

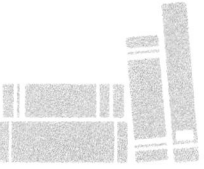

GERMINAL

. . . .

TRAGIC CLASH WITH GUARDSMEN

It is with the owners' summoning of the militia that the reader is presented with the first of the great climaxes of *Germinal* which leaves in its wake the imposition of martial law. The Montsou air is filled with unrest following the mutilation of Maigrat, and open warfare erupts during the bitter cold month of February with its backlash of police retaliation against the workers. Etienne's new role of leadership brings with it a heavy sense of despair to the reader upon the narrator's observing so closely the real plight of the miners. Amid the motifs of darkness, solitude, and nothingness, Etienne teeters on a precarious balance between sanity and madness. Hiding in Jeanlin's cave, the darkness plays upon his hyperstimulated mind as he stares into "neant tiede" / "tepid nothingness," hearing even the tiniest of noises, such as "le petit bruit d'une araingnee filant sa toile" / "the faint little sounds of a spider spinning its web" (Part VI, Ch. 1). Being an activist is not easy; Lantier is a fugitive, craving the safety of the revolutionary theoretician in some distant office. At this point, the strike has brought the already depressed economy to a standstill. We also see that Emile Zola's sympathies extended beyond the poor; they extended to a degree to the ruined small businessmen like Deneulin. Lantier begins to think as later the Bolsheviks were to think-that total revolution would be facilitated if the army were somehow to take the workers' part.

EXISTENTIALIST ALZIRE SEQUENCE

One of the saddest sequences in celebrated literature, the Alzire section in the second chapter of Part VI culminates the icy despair and pent-up wrath of the miners. It presents God and nature as irredeemably cruel and leaves us with a grieving mother in the midst of two helpless individuals-a priest and a doctor, two character-types that Albert Camus would so effectively utilize in his masterpiece of hope amid despair, *La Peste* (The Plague), in which we see the devoted and persevering figures of Father Paneloux and Dr. Rieux. Zola again used his frightening white as death-color amid the blankly matter-of-fact journalistic prose that Camus was also to utilize in the Rieux journal narrative of *La Peste*. Despite the prevalent journalese, however, there appears some exceptionally brilliant narrative penetrating little Alzire's delirious consciousness from which only incoherent murmurs emanate. The tragic victim of the abominable economic situation is given "a delirer a voix basse, riant, croyant qu'il faisait chaud et qu'elle jouait au soleil" / "to delirious murmurings incoherently laughing, believing that it would be warm and that she would be frolicking in the sunshine" (Part VI, Ch. 2). This brief shuddering passage reminds us so well of Zola's description of Bataille suffering so horribly that he has lapsed into a state of expanded consciousness. Zola's enormous debt to the Russian Naturalistic authors is patently manifest in his depictions of especially horrendous suffering, reminding us particularly of the writing of Fyodor Dostoevski.

COALESCENCE OF PLOT THEMES TOWARD THE CLIMAX

The concluding chapters of Part VI draw us to *Germinal's* irrevocable and tragic **climax** by drawing together various plot threads, beginning with the ominous spectre of the Belgian scabs who are to add the threat of humiliation to the Montsou workers to their already reduced circumstances. Parallel to the strike plot is the continuously running love-triangle involving Etienne, Chaval, and Catherine. A poignant piece of Naturalistic dialogue, from which the reader is methodically to speculate as to Etienne's and Catherine's future, anticipates Jake Barnes' and Brett Ashley's famous dialogue lamenting what might have been as they sit in a taxi at the end of *The Sun Also Rises*, so strikingly that it is almost uncanny: "Est-ce dommage, toutes ces betises? ... Nous nous serions si bien entendus!" / "Isn't it awful, all this futility? ... We would have gotten along so well together!" (Part VI, Ch. 4). It is interesting, also, that Emile Zola's *Germinal* and Ernest Hemingway's *The Sun Also Rises* both deal with the cyclical thematology of fertility and sterility. In Part VI, we also have Jeanlin's first homicide, conducted with paradoxical irrationality and yet cool resolve. We can well imagine Jeanlin as a Bakunin of the next generation, someone who can commit murder stealthily, swiftly, and without remorse. Chapter six brings with its vivid colors the tremendous eruption of an epic-scale violent confrontation in which enraged workers taunt armed guardsmen, presenting the awesome problem of riot control. The result of the clash in *Germinal* is carnage, bloodshed beyond the fathoming of the miners and the strike leaders, as a volley of gunfire bursts forth, followed by the pall of overwhelming disbelief. Contemporary recurrences of certain historic riot patterns bring periods of deceptive quiet following periods of activism as disenchanted protesters and law-enforcers today still ponder over the aftermath of similar circumstances.

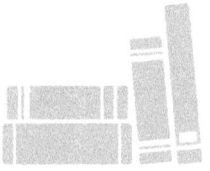

GERMINAL

. . . .

IMMEDIATE AFTERMATH

The avalanche of events following the first fatal police confrontation includes the rejection of Etienne Lantier and his disastrous leftist views by the bereaved strikers and the final ruin of Deneulin. Etienne's being turned upon by the defeated workers, now totally disenchanted by militant action, gives him to feel that even prison would offer solace. The tide of public opinion at Montsou has shifted so far that the formerly scorned Rasseneur is now in quite good standing. The innkeeper's moderate views may be attributed to the seasoning which bad experience often brings; he had become the innkeeper because he had been fired by the managers for insubordination and agitation. Deneulin's ultimate ruin comes by the same monster of big dehumanized business, which he had so ironically defended in his conservative views at the Hennebeaus' luncheon, and is masterfully described in terms of "le flot montant" / "the rising tide" (Part VII, Ch. 1) of the great corporations.

SOUVARINE'S ROLE IN THE ULTIMATE TRAGEDY

As Part VII continues, we are led to the second tragic **climax** of *Germinal* with Souvarine's sabotage of Le Voreux. Emile Zola focuses on his Souvarine colors, the whites and cold pastel shades, giving this sequence some of the most ominously apocalyptic colorations of the entire novel as we see the canal's "fuite blanche" / "white flow" amidst the "colonnades bleuies" / "blue colonnades" (Part VII, Ch. 2) of the trees. Zola used the same type of outstanding technical description in Souvarine's work underground with saw and screwdriver as he used earlier in the presentation of Le Voreux's exact mechanical specifications. Exactitude in dimensional measurements contributes to the stealthy power of the sabotage sequence: the scheme involves architectural planning, an architecture of destruction as the anarchist counts exactly fifty-four ladders down to find the crucial bulge in the fifth section's lower casing. It is at this structurally weak point that the mine shaft elevator tends to catch at three-hundred-and-seventy-four meters (twelve hundred and thirty-four feet), and it is at this point that collapse is most imminent and sabotage most concealable. As the beaten miners return to work after the violent encounter with the police, three-hundred-and-twenty-two men descend into the shaft which collapses, killing some of the men.

The primary function of the mine collapse incident is to set the miners against the labor leaders as much as the march incident set them against the police. The final description of Le Voreux collapsing on the horizon, its titanic superstructure sinking into rubble, and the interior imploding in a huge underground tremor represents Emile Zola at his best as an **epic** novelist. The author himself believed that the modern novel was the heir of Classical **epic**, and he is the celebrated master of demolitions, trainwrecks, and various other types of mechanical mishaps. Commensurate with his fathoming and grasp of vast scale, his most masterful passages are those which deal with the colossal. Among the powerful images which Zola's creative energy brought to the mine collapse passage are those of the giant whirlpool literally sucking down the rubble, of a man as struck by a cannonball, as well as such other obvious personifications as those relating to voraciousness and swallowing, and the images of the ship's mast in a hurricane and the abyss. Le Voreux is presented as a malevolent monster which has, in the manner of the Marxist forecast for capitalism, collapsed and dropped into its own hell.

PLOT DENOUEMENT: AN OVERVIEW

Part VII extends onward into a kind of **denouement**, or falling action, with a succession of still striking plot **episodes** but which basically emanate downward from Souvarine's sabotage of the mine. Another more terrible clash with the police is preceded by Souvarine's disappearance into the phantom mists of vaguely distant revolutionary rumblings, the verification of the deaths of some fifteen of the trapped miners, and the thorough embitterment of the miners' families at the total failure of the strike.

Zola has led us to an incident presented in his novel, about which he had been for some time undecided, an incident of mythic and archetypal proportions, in which we find Old Bonnemort as an almost supernatural phenomenon, rising in one last monumental effort, as the Old Testament figure of Samson rose and burst his chains to bring down the temple in his wrath. The backdrop for Zola's gruesome **episode** is a cold February day with its pale apocalyptic sun and soft blue sky, and the episodic **protagonist** is the pretty young eighteen-year-old Cecile Gregoire clad in blue to pay a charitable visit to the nearly paralyzed Bonnemort, who has lost his son as well as younger members of his family in the military police gunfire. She has, in her culpable naivete, brought a gift of some shoes for him which he can no longer use. The author's placement of blue in the scene of her first appearance in this **episode** strategically prefigures the later emergence of blue in her face. Like the other Cecile incident on the way to the Hennebeaus' party, Zola has used the quiet and tranquility of this episode's beginning to make the surprising turn of events more shuddering to us. Her first encounter out with the working people had only brought slight offense to her veil and dress, but it brings us to near shock as we look on through the omniscient narrative as an invisible bystander in the desolate hovel to see the pampered innocent cruelly strangled. And yet Zola's mastery of his theory of impartiality even sustains itself through this emotion-filled **episode**: Old Bonnemort somehow does not seem blameworthy. The succession of tragedies and slayings which have befallen his family, as well as his own paralysis, plus the mind-altering effect of forty-five years underground, places the pathetic man as a victim of circumstances, an insane but innocent man who would not have contemplated such a thing were his mind functioning normally. He is a family man, old before his years, who has suffered beyond human endurance. His action is a spontaneous involuntary paroxysm, not a premeditated act. Likewise, little Cecile, so hideously rich in the eyes of the tortured miners, is also innocent in her way as are her parents. Being conditioned as they have that their wealth is somehow determined by natural law and that they are in no way directly responsible for anyone's suffering, the Gregoires proceed on their course of ignorance and total obliviousness. Emile Zola's villain is that distant monster, that unconsciously malevolent, virulent economic godhead which, with its own scientific laws, has usurped the tabernacle. No one is personally responsible. Even the immediate cause of the final disaster, Souvarine, is a victim of circumstances in Russia: he has seen his wife executed and feels that any act of sabotage against the old order in the Bolshevik style is justified. Bent on crushing the old world, he envisions the rise of a new and better one in which workers like those of Montsou will reap their just dividends for what currently is unremunerated toil.

CONCLUSION OF "GERMINAL"

The two final chapters of the novel bring us to three powerful concluding episodes, the rescue of the Eurydice-figure Catherine by the Orpheus-figure Etienne from Chaval, the inevitable slaying of Chaval, and the profoundly terrifying passage concerning itself with Bataille. *Germinal* ends archetypally with a great flood, perhaps portending some great mythic or Biblical retribution on a world permitting such abuses. Along with this possibly Marxist washing away of the mine, Zola culminated his book with torrents of Impressionistic colorations: the reddish glow of lamps, the yellow horse, the complementary green of the rising flood with its symbolism of growth and regeneration. Before our terrified eyes, Bataille is one great apocalyptic mass of white light set against additive primary color, a frantic creature crazed by years of smothering claustrophobic confinement, lapsing into a brilliant torrent of involuntary memory as the dying animal's entire life flashes before him as he remembers "cette vision de sa jeunesse ... au souvenir confus de soleil brulant en l'air comme une grosse lampe" / "this vision of his youth... jumbled memories of the sun burning forth in the sky" (Part VII, Ch. 5). Viewing this event brings an overpoweringly existential fear to Catherine in the face of death. Etienne is ultimately rescued and disappears to join the radical Guesdist, Pluchart.

The ending of *Germinal* completes the cycle of slightly over a year: *Germinal* had begun in March and has brought us to the following April. The winter strike had lasted two and a half months, and this April signals the cruel recurrence of the life cycle of germination and death, and more immediately the cyclical return of the men to the mines with no change in the disapproved pay arrangement. We see the black again, we see "Tartaret" again, and the International Workingmen's Association in its first phase is crumbling. Zola takes us back symmetrically to the vast plain again, dashing the end of the work again with bold impasto strokes of primary color: the immense plain is suffused in "un flot d'or" / "a flood of gold"; the night mists bring "de petites nuees rouges" /" little red cloudlets"; and these cloudlets change in color to "le bleu limpide" / "limpid blue" as our eyes envision a spectral purple in the rise of a proletarian revolution "dont l'incendie embraserait la fin du siecle de cette poupre de soleil levant, qu'il regardait saigner au ciel" / "of which the flames would illuminate the new century with the purple of a rising sun, which would draw blood from the sky". The green spring signals the grim harvest of violence and ultimate revolution as we feel strange vibrations of workers beneath the trembling earth. Like the vegetation, men likewise will inevitably spring forth under the determined scientific laws of nature, economics, and most significantly, justice: "une armee noire... qui germait... grandissant pour les recoltes du siecle futur, et dont la germination allait faire bientot eclater le terre" / "a black army... which will germinate... bursting forth for the harvests of the new century, of which the germination will one day upturn the earth" (Part VII, Ch. 6).

Rather than ending *Germinal* with moral disquisitions, or with advice as to when it is most prudent to strike, or with a specific plan for the future, Zola ended his novel in a way somewhat reminiscent of his Realist precursor, Gustave

Flaubert in Madame Bovary: *Germinal* ends with basic neutrality amid counterbalanced optimism and pessimism. The novel is basically unresolved, although the pessimistic atmosphere tends to dominate much as it did in Flaubert's masterpiece. Zola presented neither moral nor practical solution; perhaps there are none. The modern technological world is, as the Positivists suggested, in a kind of third phase, a scientific phase which has grown out of and beyond the religious and the **metaphysical** phases. In the Nietzschean sense, it is a world beyond good and evil in which blind will is the life force and in which God is dead. In resolving the problem of the future, Darwin predicated his theory of natural selection on evolution through adversity, and Marx predicated his theory of revolution on the waning away or self-destruction of the old world order in terms of the adverse effects of capitalism.

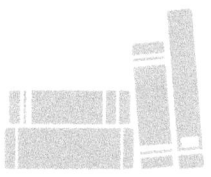

GERMINAL

....

THE GREGOIRE FAMILY

Honore Gregoire: Great-grandfather of Leon Gregoire, who made the initial investment in Montsou mine stock.

Eugenie Gregoire: Grandfather of Leon Gregoire, who inherited the mine stock purchased by his father and which, within one hundred years' time, increased in value by fivefold.

Felicien Gregoire: Father of Leon Gregoire, who inherited an enormous fortune.

Leon Gregoire: Shareholder in the Montsou Company, who lives with his wife and daughter at "La Paolaine," a lavish seven-hundred-acre estate. Living on large dividends, he is represented as an idle capitalist who is completely out of touch with the harsh realities of the mine.

Cecile Gregoire: Pampered eighteen-year-old daughter of Leon Gregoire who lives happily and obliviously at "La Paolaine," giving well intended but pathetically token charity to the poor.

She is eventually strangled by Bonnemort, a man out of his mind from misery and grief.

Deneulin: The cousin of M. Gregoire, who is the owner of Jean-Bart, a small mine which will be surrendered to the Montsou Company after the strike and its sabotage. He is a small businessman ruined by the big monopoly. He has two daughters, Jeanne and Lucie.

THE HENNEBEAU FAMILY

M. Hennebeau: Director-General of the Montsou Company, representing rich stockholders who reside in the remote security of Paris. Zola presents him masterfully as the frustrated husband of an unfaithful wife. He is the uncle of Paul Negrel.

Mme. Negrel: Sister of M. Hennebeau and mother of Paul Negrel.

Mme. Hennebeau: Hennebeau's wife and the mistress of her husband's nephew, Paul Negrel.

Paul Negrel: An engineer-foreman of Le Voreux, who has an affair with M. Hennebeau's wife, but who plans to marry Cecile Gregoire.

OTHER UNRELATED CHARACTERS REPRESENTING MANAGEMENT

Maigrat: The villainous proprietor of the Montsou Company store, despised by the workers for his demands as a creditor to the poor. He falls from a roof and is mutilated during a riot in which his store is ransacked by the militant wives led by La Brule. His name bears a striking resemblance to the French word "maigre," which means "thin," and which could be interpreted in terms of his role in starving the miners. Maigrat is depicted as a greedy self-indulgent coward.

Vanderhagen: The Montsou Company doctor with the hopeless job of tending to the ill and injured.

THE MAHEU FAMILY

Guillaume Mahue: Great-grandfather of Toussaint Maheu.

Nicholas Maheu: Grandfather of Toussaint Maheu.

Bonnemort: Vincent Maheu (father of Toussaint Maheu): A former underground hauler who presently works as a wagon-tender on the surface. He has black lung disease, chronic acute bronchitis, which causes him to cough up coal dust. He has worked in the mines for forty-five years and must still work, despite the fact that he is an invalid, so that he will be entitled to his pension. His nickname "Bonnemort" is indicative of his ability to perpetually escape death and survive in the mines. He finally loses his mind and strangles Cecile Gregoire after the Montsou killings, afterward losing his pension and turning into a vegetable.

Toussaint Maheu: Son of Bonnemort, married to La Maheude. He is a Voreux hauler killed by the guardsmen in the police confrontation at the end of the strike.

Constance (La) Maheude: Wife of Toussaint Maheu. Determined not to weaken during the strike, she becomes increasingly bitter and resigned to her fate. She goes to work down in the mine herself after the strike to feed her surviving children, Alzire, Catherine, and Zacharie, after the death of her husband.

Zacharie Maheu: The twenty-one-year-old eldest son of the Maheus, who marries Philomene Lavaque. He is killed in a firedamp explosion while rescuing his sister Catherine and Etienne.

Catherine Maheu: The fourteen-year-old second child of the Maheus who is an underground cart tender and the mistress of the cruel Chaval. She loves Etienne Lantier, but he has come too late for her.

Jeanlin Maheu: The eleven-year-old third child of the Maheus who becomes a child criminal, hiding in an abandoned mine shaft and eventually murdering the young soldier, Jules.

Alzire Maheu: The sadly appealing eight-year-old fourth child of the Maheus who is a hunchback and ultimately dies during the strike of cold and starvation.

Leonore Maheu: Six-year-old fifth child of the Maheus.

Henri Maheu: Four-year-old sixth child of the Maheus.

Estelle Maheu: Seventh child of the Maheus.

OTHER CHARACTERS REPRESENTING LABOR

Levaque: Voreux hauler who is a neighbor of the Maheus. His wife plays mistress to their boarder, Bouteloup. Their nineteen-year-old daughter, Philomene, is the mistress and wife of Zacharie Maheu, and has two children, Achille and Desiree.

Bebert: A pit boy killed at the end of the strike, he is Philomene's twelve-year-old brother.

Louis Bouteloup: A timber cutter for mine casings, who lives with the Levaques.

La Brule: The mother of La Pierronne and the widow of a hauler killed in the mine. She becomes a confirmed revolutionary, and she is finally killed in the confrontation between the miners and the military police.

Pierron: A Voreux miner who avoids joining the strikers.

La Pierronne: The daughter of La Brule, the wife of Pierron, and the mistress of the foreman Dansaert.

Lydie Pierron: Pierron's ten-year-old daughter who is a playmate of Jeanlin and Bebert. She is a child laborer along with many of the other children and is killed in the riot.

Etienne Lantier: Zola's **protagonist** in *Germinal*, descended from the Macquart family through the laundress of *L'Assommoir* and the courtesan *Nana*. He is an outsider, through whose consciousness much of the narrative flows, and is given to sudden incipient rages which are vaguely linked to an affinity to alcohol and to the "lesion organique" which accurses Zola's families. Etienne avoids alcohol, vaguely realizing some hereditary weakness to its effects. Lantier is a Voreux hauler hired by the Montsou Company after being fired from the railroad for insubordination. He becomes the leader of the strike, develops vague and unsynthesized Marxist leanings, and seems at times to be a voice for Zola. After the suppression of the strike by martial law, Lantier leaves Montsou and goes to Paris evidently to further pursue revolutionary causes.

Cheval: A Voreux hauler who is the rival against Lantier for Catherine. He is brutal to Catherine, who is basically afraid of him. He crosses the strike line to work for a Voreux rival, and at the end, is killed by Lantier in an underground fight.

Pluchart: He is a former mechanic who is the secretary of the Northern Federation of the International Workingmen's Association. He functions as an ideological Marxist mentor for Lantier in the story.

Rasseneur: He is the innkeeper-proprietor of "L'Avantage" in Montsou near Le Voreux. A former miner himself, who was fired for arousing agitation among the workers, he is a popular moderate leftist gradualist-type Socialist leader among the miners. Rasseneur and Lantier become leadership rivals, Lantier being the more radical and the more immediately successful of the two. Mme. Rasseneur tends to be more radical than her husband, as well.

Souvarine: Nihilistic Russian emigrant who espouses not just the Marxist ideology of the extreme left, but who is an anarchist of the Bolshevik type. He is a Voreux machinist and sabotages the mine casings as an advocate of direct militant action. Zola seems to have included him in the novel as perhaps the major factor in the strike's ending so badly, with the repressed workers returning to work again worse off than they were before and under the same pay-arrangement against which they originally protested. In addition to their having to return to work, they have to mourn their dead, and they have to repair the wrecked mines.

Mouque: An old former miner who is a comrade of Bonnemort.

Mouquette: The daughter of Mouque, who is eventually killed in the uprising. She is robustly jolly, quite plump, and vulgarly defiant.

Berloque: (Chicot): A miner killed by a collapse and slide.

Desir: Widow who holds the Bon-Joyeux ball and who sets up her ballroom for the assembly of striking miners.

Quandieu: A senior mine foreman.

Abbe Ranvier: The Cure of Montsou who succeeds the Abbe Joire. He is a Christian Socialist and is eventually replaced by the Bishop.

Bataille: A horse killed in the Voreux mine flood after having lived at the bottom of the pit for ten years. His yellow color contributes to his role as an apocalyptic spectre.

Trompette: Another horse taken to the bottom of the mine pit, but which survives for only a few months.

Poland: Rasseneur's pet rabbit, which he has tamed.

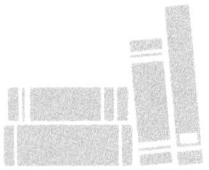

GERMINAL

. . . .

REPUTATION AND INFLUENCE

Even though virtually all the novels and stories which Emile Zola wrote were commercial successes, the author's reputation has fluctuated since his own lifetime. With regard to Zola's involvement in the Dreyfus Affair, it has been almost unanimously agreed that the writer of "J' Accuse" was correct in his appraisal of the military and of the unfortunate Jew convicted and later acquitted of treason. From the standpoint of his literature, however, Emile Zola's reputation began to disintegrate after his death with only a few of the Rougon-Macquart novels holding sustained readership. The novels of the cycle to dwindle most rapidly in acclaim were those concerned with the bourgeoisie. The ones to attain lasting reputations were the powerful working-class novels. For a long time, *L' Assommoir* (The Drinking Establishment) and *Nana* were the most widely read of Zola's slum stories. Recently, however, *Germinal* has ascended to the summit in scholarly research, critical acclaim, and general readership.

Near the turn of the century, it was believed that Zola's brand of Naturalism was moribund as a literary school. Many critics believed that it was so rigid and of such limited scope that its resources would exhaust quickly and that, artistically, it was virtually a dead end. Critics to concur with this point of view included Ferdinand Brunetiere, who wrote on the bankruptcy of Naturalism as a system and technique, and the five young writers who wrote their "Manifesto of the Five" as a polemic against the hardened Naturalism of *La Terre* (The Earth).

NOTOREITY IN ENGLAND

It was the novel *La Terre* (The Earth) which secured for the author a degree of notoriety in England, where the National Vigilance Association, an organized group of Victorian fanatics, successfully suppressed English translations of the Rougon-Macquart novels by having a prominent publisher brought up before criminal court and sentenced to jail. *La Terre* (The Earth), the bitter story dealing with the conditions under which poverty-stricken peasant farmers lived, has a climactic sequence which was considered obscene in earlier times.

Because Emile Zola's actual technique was actually more sophisticated than his simplistic scientific theory, he received acclaim from writers other than those of the Naturalist schools. Because of his tendency toward poetic symbolism, Zola received acclaim from such French poets as Theophile Gautier and Stephane Mallarme. In England, where he had earlier received so much scorn, he was to receive acclaim by Henry James and Havelock Ellis. The latter, a now-celebrated but then-controversial psychologist, not only translated *Germinal* into English but predicted that it would survive all of the other Rougon-Macquart novels in the twentieth century.

"GERMINAL" IN FOREGROUND TODAY

Today, it is *Germinal* upon which Emile Zola's reputation basically rests, a novel being reexamined for its modernist artistic and political leanings. Even though the eminent Marxist critic George Lukacs condemned *Germinal* for its neutrality and seeming lack of commitment, it has nevertheless become the subject of much contemporary Marxist research. Primarily, however, it is the Expressionist and apocalyptic characteristic of the novel that is bringing it to the foreground in the world of letters today.

Frequently overlooked is a very fine short story of Emile Zola from the Medan authors' collection, *Les Soirees de Medan*, which concerns itself with the Franco-Prussian War. Frequently included in anthologies on both the secondary school level and the college level, "L'Attaque de Moulin" / "The Attack on the Mill" is often the first story of Emile Zola's with which the student of French or English has contact.

Even though the novels of Emile Zola have for some time been considered to be inferior to the works of other contemporary authors (Gustave Flaubert, Guy de Maupassant, Leo Tolstoi, Ivan Turgenev, Fyodor Dostoevski), it is becoming increasingly evident in retrospect that Emile Zola's influence on subsequent authors has cast a shadow from the nineteenth century nearly as long as that cast by Marcel Proust in the twentieth.

ZOLA'S INFLUENCE IN AMERICA

With regard to the influence of Zola on subsequent novelists, we may note that his influence has not been confined solely to European contemporaries, but, in fact, has spread to many

American novelists as well, especially between the two World Wars. In the United States, we may take particular notice of the novels of what Gertrude Stein referred to as the "lost generation." In the period of the Depression, when leftist sentiment became an inherent part of our society, it was inevitable that some form of Marxism would manifest itself in the novel as well. Zola's American Naturalistic heirs include Frank Norris, Theodore Dreiser, Upton Sinclair, John Dos Passos, Erskine Caldwell, and James T. Farrell.

Despite adverse criticism from the English Victorian establishment, Zola influenced such English authors as George Moore and John Galsworthy. On the Continent, his more obvious heirs include such French authors as Guy de Maupassant, Joris Karl Huysmans, and Jules Romains, and such German authors as Hermann Sudermann and Gerhart Hauptmann. In spite of the profuse adverse criticism Zola received in Europe, such as that leveled against him by Ferdinand Brunetiere in his declaration that Zola's Naturalism was virtually bankrupt, his influence went so far as August Strindberg's Sweden and Maxim Gorki's Russia as early as the end of the nineteenth century.

Once Naturalism had appeared to have run its course in Europe by the end of the nineteenth century, it came to the United States in the early part of the twentieth century and then back to Europe again with the influx of a unique American strain. The most Zola-like of the American Naturalists were the hard Naturalists like Frank Norris (*The Octopus*), Upton Sinclair (*King Coal*, *The Jungle*), Jack London (*The Iron Heel*) and Theodore Dreiser (*An American Tragedy*, part of which appears to be transparently similar to Zola's *Therese Raquin*). It was only after World War I that the leftist sympathies of these authors drew their popularity to Europe, especially to Soviet Russia, which revealed in inferences that the United States was the victim of runaway capitalism. The greatest masterpieces of American Naturalism revealed a blend of the European determinism spawned by Darwin, Comte, and Marx, plus the fresh new blood of American genius in character-building and regional environmentalism. Works in this category reversed the direction of the influence-trend back to Europe again from America.

The outstanding novelists of the new American Naturalist school had that unique hardness that so many had earlier found reprehensible in Emile Zola's controversial works. These novelists included a group of Europe-influenced liberals who influenced subsequent U. S. Naturalist literature immeasurably, influencing such documenters of the Sacco-Vanzetti controversy as Upton Sinclair (*Boston*), John Dos Passos (*Big Money*), and Maxwell Anderson (*Winterset*). Naturalist documentation of such **themes** as the Spanish Civil War, the leftist cause, and pro-Russia sympathy appears repeatedly in such books as Ernest Hemingway's *Fifth Column*, John Dos Passos' *Adventures of a Young Man*, Granville Hicks' *Only One Storm*, and Maxwell Anderson's *Key Largo*. Among the Zola-heirs of American Naturalism to acquire momentous fame in Europe during the crucial time between the two World Wars were Ernest Hemingway, John Steinbeck, and William Faulkner. Steinbeck's work bears an unmistakable Zolaesque lyricism amid brutality, and such works as *Of Mice and Men* bear the archetypal grimness and compassion that can be observed in Zola's best working-class novels. *The Grapes of Wrath* is a work of Zolaesque sociological Naturalism, with its pronounced sympathy to the left and its catastrophes attributable to heredity, environment, and the economic system. *In Dubious Battle* is somewhat reminiscent of *Germinal* with its thematic problems of labor-management relations involving strikes, lockouts, and civil unrest.

We are currently entering a period in history in which a rediscovery of Zola, as both a commentator and an artist, is taking a principal place in the world of letters. Contemporary twentieth-century scholars, in many cases, are belatedly examining fiction as the rhetoric of a given period rather than examining it exclusively in terms of literary form. In fact, whatever artistic shortcomings Emile Zola's novels may admittedly possess are more than offset by the novels' power and preeminence as diversified nineteenth-century French rhetoric. Literature in the tradition of Emile Zola has come into its own in the post-Symbolist / post-Expressionist era of a grim new kind of non-fiction novel, reportage of the sort that we associate with the modern journalese novelists and the modern chroniclers of contemporary history. Zola has the original novelist of the press, and it was to those novelists of Europe and America who were and are journalists, editors, and correspondents that his brand of rhetorical. Naturalism was so perfectly suited.

ZOLA IN ENGLISH TRANSLATION

In spite of the fact that some of the best research on Emile Zola that exists today has been pursued in the English language, including that by Elliott M. Grant (which actually appears in French translation in Gallimard's authoritative annotated text), Emile Zola's Rougon-Macquart novels originally received a most inhospitable reception in the English-speaking world.

As inconceivable as it might seem today, Zola's original English translator was actually fined and sentenced to prison for publishing works of the Rougon-Macquart cycle in English. What is even more inconceivable is that the English translations were so abridged in the interest of Victorian pseudo-modesty that they could scarcely be called translations at all; and to crown the issue, no effort was ever made to curtail Emile Zola's works in the original French.

To cast some light on this bizarre story, it must be understood that, from around 1860 up into the 1880s, general anti-French sentiment was running rampant in Victorian England. A haughty sentiment of English superiority in matters dealing with morality made her stand in particularly harsh judgment of controversial foreign books, while many of her own were equally if not more objectionable by these same fanatical puritan standards. England's way of suggesting moral inferiority on the part of the French was to forbid translation of controversial French novels like Gustave Flaubert's *Madame Bovary* and Zola's *Rougon-Macquart* while at the same time allowing them to circulate freely throughout England in French.

The course of events concerning the controversial translations of the Zola novels into English basically went as follows. Henry Vizetelly, a devote of French literature and a frequent visitor to Paris, had the benefit of being descended from a long line of printers and decided to venture upon English translations of the commercially successful Rougon-Macquart novels. Having barely begun in the business of publishing fiction with some of George Moore's work and a few works by French authors such as Alphonse Daudet, Prosper Merimee, and George Sand, Vizetelly decided to embark on the admittedly daring Zola venture, considering the Victorian climate of late nineteenth-century England.

Henry Vizetelly began his ill-fated succession of Zola translation with *Therese Raquin*, *La Curee* (translated as The Rush for the Spoil), and *Pot-Bouille* (translated as Piping Hot) with introductions by the ardent Zola supporter, George Moore. The most daring aspects of the whole Zola enterprise were the translations of *Nana* and *La Terre* (translated as Soil).

It was particularly with *Soil* that Vizetelly began to receive the relentless bad press that continued unceasingly to harass him in such esteemed publications as *The Fortnightly Review*, which brought confiscation of the translations by English library authorities from the public shelves. Despite the fact that George Moore was outraged by this form of censorship and argued that literature was not for purposes of moralizing alone, the anti-Zola sentiment reached the public at large, primarily through the press and such organizations as the National Vigilance Association.

Once the National Vigilance Association established its merciless pursuit of the Zola controversy, it was not long until it reached the halls of the House of Commons in open debate. With the matter before the English government, and the public in an uproar, prosecution proceedings were begun and preparations made for trial against Vizetelly. He attempted to defend himself on the grounds that parts of the Bible, sequences from Shakespeare's plays, and even certain revered English classics would be similarly condemned if judged under the same strict standards imposed on Emile Zola's work. This defense was overruled, however, and Henry Vizetelly was fined one hundred pounds.

Shortly thereafter, Vizetelly was again prosecuted, this time with precedent against him, for pursuing further translations of other Rougon-Macquart novels such as *La Ventre de Paris* (translated as Fat and Thin), *La Joie de Vivre* (How Jolly Life Is!), and *La Faute de L'Abbe Mouret* (Abbe Mouret's Transgression), as well as Gustave Flaubert's *Madame Bovary* and two celebrated short stories of Guy de Maupassant. This time, he was not only fined by the court but was sentenced to three months in jail for inability to pay the fine. Efforts by distinguished writers to secure Vizetelly's release were unsuccessful. Henry Vizetelly's business, as well as his health, were ruined by this unfortunate sequence of events. His son, Ernest Alfred Vizetelly, was to write a fine biography of Emile, Zola defending Zola to the utmost, in years to come. This same biography has been recently reissued in a new edition.

With the end of Victorianism, there came in England a pronounced rise of Emile Zola's works in critical favor. Among those Englishmen who were to give their support to Zola's writings were such men of letters as Havelock Ellis and Henry James. In retrospect, one must admire the courage of Henry Vizetelly which cost him so dearly in business, reputation, and health. He shared a degree of courage against the establishment similar to that shown by Zola in the ugly and controversial Dreyfus Affair.

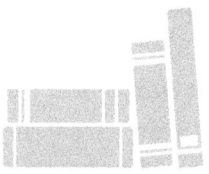

GERMINAL

. . . .

The following examination questions are basic stock questions that the student of *Germinal* should expect to receive in an ordinary essay examination. The answers are basic skeletal answers which could in some cases be elaborated upon by the student depending on time factors.

In judiciously anticipating other stock questions, the student might extrapolate other questions and answers from the other sections of this volume. In such cases, the commentator would be indulging in repetition to include them in this section.

Question: Discuss the general philosophical trends of the post-1848 generation as they apply to *Germinal*.

Answer: In rooting out the general philosophical trends of the post-1848 generation, we may concern ourselves with Auguste Comte's brand of Positivism; Hippolyte Taine's scientific criticism applying the elements of heredity, environment, and period to literature; Charles Darwin's theory of natural selection; and Karl Marx's scientific interpretation of revolution.

In examining Comte's Positivistic philosophy, one may see in *Germinal* that Christianity appears to be nearly exhausted of its inspirational resources amidst the scientific and deterministic forces around Montsou. The church is a begrimed edifice, blending into the dull grey of Montsou, and the Abbe Joire avoids any special commitments to the mining community. When Alzire dies, God actually seems cruel. Zola's recurrent "tabernacle" image, relating to the malevolent forces of Capitalism, is suggestive of the ascendancy of Comte's third scientific phase over the first two, the religious and the metaphysical.

Darwinism is manifest in *Germinal* through the preeminence of environmental adversity in the shaping of the miners' resistances and potentialities. Continued oppression will force the next generation of miners up through the earth in the same way that things turn a spectral white from continued darkness. Generation succeeds generation, the hereditary strain adapting itself and improving in strength from the forces around it.

The scientific view of history embraced by Marx is basically an extension of Darwin's theory of evolution, emerging as a more radical theory of revolution. On a cosmic social-political scale, Marx's philosophy is an ideology of change encompassing the idea that a new world will emerge by natural economic laws and that one of these natural laws is the inevitable self-destruction of capitalism. Examples of this seemingly inherent destructibility are somewhat vague in *Germinal* because Zola's proletarian revolution is placed in some distant future. The dramatic **climax**, with the mine shaft of Le Voreux falling in upon itself, however, portends Marxist-style revolution. One can observe the various types of Marxist disciples among the characters of *Germinal* as well: Etienne, Rasseneur, Pluchart, Souvarine.

Question: Discuss Emile Zola's use of spectral color effects in Impressionistic technique in *Germinal*.

Answer: In the manner of the late nineteenth-century Impressionists, Emile Zola created spectral color effects, effectively perceived by deduction through primary color adjacencies, in *Germinal* by placing red, blue, green, or yellow in various combinations in his descriptive passages. The Impressionists were highly aware of the scientific and technical properties of color, focusing particularly on unique interactions between primary colors. Being basically objective and imbued with the mentality of "scientisme," the Impressionists would place patches of vivid primary color adjacent to one another and allow the cultivated "innocent eye" neutrality of the Impressionistic mind's eye to put the colors together in spectral combination. Rather than actually mixing the primary colors, the Impressionists allowed the viewers to create these spectral effects. Some of these primary color arrangements might interact additively to yield spectral white light, and some might interact subtractively to yield spectral black.

One may cite numerous passages in *Germinal* containing combination of red, blue, green, or yellow-set against white light or black. Sometimes a spectral effect of purple might appear with the apparent mingling of red and blue, as at the end of the story. Numerous mine scenes contain red fires, blue gasses, and glimpses of the yellow horse against a black backdrop. In the apocalyptic passages, the yellow horse is almost like white light, a phosphorescent mass enhanced in its spectral character by the surrounding color combinations. Often black and white are treated as opposites of the same ominous prophecies embodied in color.

Such scenes in *Germinal* as the village panorama highlighting the multitude of small houses, and the picture of Rasseneur's inn trimmed in the primaries, exude the spirit and mentality of Impressionism. In places, Zola even goes beyond Impressionism to Surrealism and Expressionism in the apocalyptic visions and his treatment of animals. The most obvious examples of this type of material appear in the sequence describing Jeanlin's underground cave and in the sequences involving Bataille, especially that during the final flood.

Question: Discuss Emile Zola's debt to Classicism in *Germinal*.

Answer: In the most fundamental sense, Zola was indebted to the mythic fertility-death motif in not only the title of *Germinal* but in the ominously cyclical story as well. Thematology as well as **imagery** relating to the processes of procreation and germination, such as reference to the grain goddess Ceres and prolonged sequences dealing with large families, abound in the novel.

Other mythic references in *Germinal* include the likening of Le Voreux to a Cyclops, the oblique reference to Tartarus, and the obvious reworking of the Kronos-Uranus story. The entire realm of business enterprise reminds us of some labyrinth, and the malevolent crouched god to which Zola alludes reminds us of the Classical minotaur. As well as being of a basically mythic fabric content-wise, *Germinal* bears characteristics of the Homeric **epic** form-wise. In addition to giving us a sense of vast **epic** scale, the author utilizes a form of repetition (sometimes to an excess) similar to that in the ancient oral epics. The dragging of the villainous Maigrat in the dirt reminds us vaguely, in its sense of retribution, of Achilles' dragging Hector in the dirt at the end of the *Iliad*. The **theme** of retribution is also manifest in Zola's numerous **allusions** to fires and strange subterranean volcanoes.

Emile Zola's debt to Classicism also reveals a predilection for the unities and plot devices of the tragedies. **Exposition** by elder miners comes to us in the manner of the choric ode, and plot advances in a clearly defined episodic pattern, complete with complication, crisis, **climax**, and denouement. Etienne's personal defeat comes in a powerful turn of events reminiscent of the Classical "peripeteia" in which fortune reverses-as Lantier's crowd rises beyond his control and the villagers hold him responsible for the slaughter which befalls them at the hands of the guardsmen. Lantier's tragic flaw might, perhaps, be his ambition to accomplish more than what his fragmentary theoretical background and insurmountable obstacles can yield. This is where one can observe the distinction between Naturalistic tragedy and Classical tragedy: in Zola's *Germinal*, circumstances are determined by natural laws and are, as yet, beyond the characters' individual or collective control.

9 781645 421061